'WILL THERE BE FREE WILL IN HEAVEN?'

'WILL THERE BE FREE WILL IN HEAVEN?'

Freedom, Impeccability and Beatitude

SIMON FRANCIS GAINE OP

T & T CLARK
A Continuum imprint
LONDON • NEW YORK

T&T CLARK LTD

A Continuum imprint

The Tower Building   370 Lexington Avenue
11 York Road   New York
London SE1 7NX   NY 10017–6503

www.continuumbooks.com

First published 2003

ISBN 0 567 08950 9

British Library Cataloguing-in-Publication Data
A catalogue record for this book is available from the British Library

Typeset by Waverley Typesetters, Galashiels
Printed and bound in Great Britain by
Biddles Ltd, Guildford and King's Lynn

Contents

Foreword

One of the perennial questions in Christian theology, for people who believe in God as well as for those who don't, is how to say something sensible about the relationship between God's freedom and ours.

If something happens it is tempting to think either that God brought it about or that we did so. As Thomas Aquinas noted (*Summa Contra Gentiles*, book 3, chapter 70), 'it seems difficult for some people to understand how natural effects are attributed to God and to a natural agent'. He was surely being polite. Most of us, if not all, are tempted to picture the relationship between God and ourselves in competitive terms.

If we attribute whatever good we do to God, as we surely should, it begins to look as if what we do, being entirely God's work, must only be an empty show. Worse, we look like puppets, manipulated by God, moving us like pieces on a chess board, perhaps even quite arbitrarily.

Alternatively, if we attribute what we do to ourselves, emphasising our free will and personal responsibility, it becomes difficult to understand what there is for God to contribute. Very easily we are tempted into regarding God as at best the one who gave us our freedom in the first place but who must now sit on the sidelines and watch how we exercise it. Down this line, God soon becomes redundant.

Either we are free or God is free, so it seems. It takes thought to break out of the grip of this very natural way of picturing the relationship between us and God in terms of some kind of competition, as if we and God were rivals, on the same plane.

One of the many implications of this natural tendency to misconceive the relationship between divine and human freedom is to take it for granted that, if we have chosen God once and for all, we are no longer free. Even in other relationships it is easy to think like this. As regards the bond of marriage, for example, there is a temptation to talk as if the spouses were no longer free unless each was renewing the covenanted relationship between them every minute of the day or at any rate at regular intervals. We seem not to be acting freely unless we could always be acting differently and indeed contrariwise. It is as if we could only be doing the right thing if we were constantly suppressing the desire to do the opposite.

The test case, here, is focused on the psychological state of the saints in heaven. While they cannot be totally absorbed in contemplating the goodness of God for all eternity unless they have been granted the grace of doing so freely, it is significant that we often hear people saying that being in heaven must be very 'boring'. Behind that no doubt quite superficial and only half serious complaint there surely lies this same difficulty of understanding how divine and human freedom relate to one another. Once again, if the blessed in heaven are held now for all eternity in God's love, so that there is no possibility of their disengaging themselves, it is tempting to say they cannot be 'free'. If they can no longer choose some other course of action than enjoying the beatific vision – if they no longer have the possibility of sinning – it can easily look as if this means that they no longer have sovereignty over their own free will.

Of course, when we put it like this, we soon remember that free will is not like this. In the case of marriage, for example, we know that a couple can be growing in the freedom of their promises to each other without having to keep excluding temptations to infidelity. All the time, in everyday life, we act perfectly freely without there being any alternative. That we do often have to grit our teeth and act as we say almost against our will, does not mean that we are never exercising our freedom unless we are simultaneously resisting this or that temptation to sin.

In heaven the saints are not like puppets. That sin is by definition no longer a possibility for them does not deprive them

of the autonomy and self-determination which are so essential
to human life. On the contrary, the once and for all conformity
between the saint's will and the divine will is the paradigm of
the fulfilment of human freedom.

These are the questions about the relationship between divine
and human freedom that have occupied philosophers and
theologians for centuries. In this book we are introduced to great
Catholic theologians, like Francisco Suárez, John Duns Scotus,
William of Ockham, and especially Thomas Aquinas, and in
particular to their different and conflicting attempts to account
for the freedom of the saints in heaven. The scholarship and
analytical skill with which their theories are expounded enable
us to focus on the perennially important questions which
engaged them, and which continue to engage us, in the never-
ending struggle to understand the nature of human freedom,
and the relationship between created and divine freedom.

FERGUS KERR OP

Acknowledgements

I am very grateful to Dr Richard Cross for reading an early draft of Chapters 1 to 5, and for his kind and helpful suggestions, but I should add that the book is not his fault! I should also like to express my thanks to Fr Vivian Boland OP, Fr Timothy John Calvert OP, Fr Peter Hunter OP, Fr Fergus Kerr OP, Fr Denis Minns OP and Fr Richard Joseph Ounsworth OP.

SIMON FRANCIS GAINE OP

1

'Will there Be Free Will in Heaven?'

Just before Christmas 1999, various prominent public figures, teachers, clergymen and others received a set of ten questions from the BBC's *Today* programme. Nine of the ten questions were perhaps rather predictable, asking whether the recipients believed the world was created in seven days, whether the virgin birth and resurrection were literally true, and so on. One of the questions was, however, a little more unusual: Will there be free will in heaven? In reply to an email sent by me to the *Today* programme to ask how this particular question had come to be chosen, the producer Rod Liddle wrote that he himself had thought up the questions. He added that they were all 'motivated by nothing more profound than the curiosity' he had had since childhood. On the question of free will in heaven, he recorded that, of the clergy who answered, most 'didn't have much more of a clue' than he himself did. He said however that they were 'split on the issue'. In other words, some thought there would be free will in heaven, while others thought not. There was also what he called 'the inevitable quibbling over the definition of "free will"'. And he concludes: 'The closest we got to a consensus was the view which could be roughly summarised as: "Yes, there's free will, but you wouldn't *want* to do the wrong thing."'

This 'nearest-to-a-consensus' reveals what was really being asked when Liddle's question about free will in heaven was put: the respondents were being asked whether the blessed, that is, the inhabitants of heaven, were able to do the 'wrong thing', that is, to *sin*. Liddle's clergymen may have been divided

1

WRONG

or simply confused, but the traditional Christian answer is that the blessed *cannot* sin, cannot want to sin, but instead are impeccable. However, if they are unable to sin, the problem raised is whether this inability makes them less free than they were on earth, where sin was in contrast a real possibility for them. These are the issues raised by Liddle's question. However, such issues seem not to be among the central concerns either of philosophers of religion or of theologians. When the philosophers J. L. Mackie and Antony Flew, in separate arguments against the 'free will defence' of God's goodness and omnipotence in the face of evil, presented the possibility of a world of perfect free choices created by God, neither made any attempt to draw any comparison with the Christian notion of heaven.[1] Philosophers of religion in general seem to show little interest in eschatological issues other than immortality and the possibility of an 'afterlife', and where heaven is a main point of discussion the question of heavenly impeccability and freedom is usually either not explicitly treated or not even explicitly raised.[2]

Often philosophers seem more interested in hell than they are in heaven. For example, in the chapter of the Blackwell *A Companion to Philosophy of Religion* assigned to 'Heaven and Hell',[3] Jonathan L. Kvanvig devotes much of his chapter to the question of the justice of hell, which he takes to be the fundamental issue about hell for Christian thought. When he turns to the notion of heaven, he notes a few issues which he says are discussed by Christians, but goes on himself to ask about the justice of heaven just as he has spent most of his

---

[1]   J. L. Mackie, 'Evil and Omnipotence', *Mind* 64 (1955), pp. 200–12; A. Flew, 'Divine Omnipotence and Human Freedom', in A. Flew and A. Macintyre, *New Essays in Philosophical Theology* (London: SCM Press, 1955), pp. 144–69, esp. pp. 149–60. L. Moonan, 'Theodicy and Blissful Freedom', *New Blackfriars* 80 (1999), pp. 502–11, supposes Flew to have made reference to the 'theologian's notion'. In fact Flew speaks of the beatific vision of heaven only with respect to its being a state of reward rather than in comparison to his own notion of a world of perfect free choices.
[2]   See e.g. J. Hick, *Death and Eternal Life* (London: Macmillan, 1976), esp. p. 206.
[3]   P. L. Quinn and C. Taliaferro (eds), *A Companion to Philosophy of Religion* (Cambridge, MA and Oxford: Blackwell, 1997), pp. 562–8.

chapter on the justice of hell. His list of questions about heaven includes whether one can leave heaven once one is there. This question is related to the (distinct) question of impeccability in heaven, since one could imagine that sin might be one way – though by no means the only way – by which heaven might be lost. Other ways might include a divine decree simply to remove someone.

The questions concerning heavenly impeccability and freedom are, nevertheless, addressed occasionally by a philosopher of religion, and then normally only in passing. However, where such questions are addressed at greater length, they seem to have given rise to extreme positions, involving the rejection of impeccability in their accounts of heaven. For example, there are the opinions expressed in 1977 and 1985 by George B. Wall[4] and his critic, John Donnelly,[5] respectively. While Wall holds that the blessed in heaven would be unfree if they were impeccable, Donnelly wants to maintain the freedom of the blessed by denying their impeccability. The views propounded by Wall and Donnelly serve to show the tension between notions of freedom and impeccability that make Liddle's question an interesting, divisive and confusing one.

Wall's purpose is to argue that doubts about God's goodness raised by the problem of evil cannot be resolved by recourse to the concept of 'heaven', a concept which in fact only compounds the problem. He writes that whatever the Christian conception of heaven involves, it will involve the absence of moral evil. The explanation he gives of this absence is that 'freedom is jettisoned in heaven'.[6] According to Wall, this raises problems for the defence of God's goodness: Since heaven is meant to be a better state than earth, and heaven in contrast to earth is without freedom, why did this good God not create such a heavenly unfree world on earth instead of this one?

Having dealt thus with what he takes to be the Christian notion of heaven, Wall goes on to develop what he sees as an

---

[4] G. B. Wall, 'Heaven and a Wholly Good God', *Personalist* 58 (1977), pp. 352–7.
[5] J. Donnelly, 'Eschatological Enquiry', *Sophia* 24 (1985), pp. 16–31.
[6] Wall, 'Heaven and a Wholly Good God', p. 352.

alternative notion of heaven, which should be considered as possibly doing a better job in the defence of God's goodness. Taking up the suggestion that a world with a temporary pre-heavenly freedom would be better than one totally without, he counters that a world with permanent freedom, heavenly as well as earthly, would surely be better still. He argues that 'moral perfection' is better than its absence and should therefore be sustained in heaven. Heaven will therefore require the continuation of freedom for the sake of moral perfection: without freedom heaven (presumably the Christian heaven) would be 'an amoral state in which moral perfection is impossible'. Moreover if striving for moral perfection rather than its achievement is taken as what is good, this striving and its conditions should be retained in heaven.

Assuming then a notion of heaven in which freedom survives, Wall asks why a good God did not bring in this state from the beginning. The best answer to this, he says, is that moral perfection in heaven requires freedom, which in turn requires the possibility of moral evil. A pre-heavenly life would thus be necessarily envisaged in which one acquires the virtues necessary for the loving relationships of heaven that give rise to bliss. When one has learned the value of such virtue, one will never turn away from it but forever freely seek to express the virtues one has acquired.[7] Wall, however, doubts that any preparation can really secure such irreversible expression of truth and love. He writes, 'As long as the inhabitants of heaven remain free, does not reversal of character remain a possibility?'[8] The view that knowledge will guarantee virtue is taken to be 'Socratic' rather than Christian; moreover it is 'questionable on psychological grounds'. Wall suggests that 'heaven' might be modified to a conditional state 'from which a person could freely slip' into a purgatory where the virtues required for heaven could be redeveloped. Nevertheless Wall finds problems even with such a view: Why did a good God not create such a purgatory rather than earth as a prelude to heaven, if purgatory is so much better at what he calls 'virtue-installation'? It seems

[7]   Wall, 'Heaven and a Wholly Good God', p. 353.
[8]   Wall, 'Heaven and a Wholly Good God', p. 354.

that for Wall, no heaven will do, neither the one he takes to be Christian nor the one of his own devising.

In a reply to this article, John Donnelly writes that Wall seems to believe that his arguments will encourage rationally minded Christians to abandon an 'orthodox' notion of heaven as excluding moral evil. Donnelly, however, supposes that Wall is incorrect in attributing the absence of moral evil in heaven to 'orthodox Christianity'. Evidently committed to the value of Christian orthodoxy, he attempts to counter Wall's argument against heaven by denying that the orthodox notion of heaven entails an absence of evil, developing a notion of heaven similar to Wall's alternative notion but asserting its Christian orthodoxy. He writes, 'To think that when one attains heaven, due to the achievement of some degree of moral perfection, one no longer needs to be free, is to misunderstand the Christian notion of heaven.'[9]

On Donnelly's view, the inhabitants of heaven are endlessly subject to the command to be perfect as an ongoing, progressive task. This view of heaven is one that involves freedom and therefore the real possibility of moral evil. The possible moral evils in a heavenly resurrection would include 'personal offences', Donnelly's examples being the 'immoral sentiments of pride, jealousy, envy, hatred', and possibly the 'ordinary range of vices' that might otherwise cause innocent suffering from concomitant natural evils, were God not to prevent such harms in this case from coming about. Donnelly describes this state of affairs as 'a kind of ethical intentionalism . . . under the scrutiny of an omniscient Deity' and happily accepts the implication that heaven might be lost through sin (and possibly but not necessarily regained).[10]

Donnelly's method of procedure in establishing the orthodoxy of his own view is not the consultation of any ecclesiastical authorities (which, in any case, would give him no support). Instead two considerations seem to be at work: God's respect for human freedom, and the fall of Satan and his followers. Donnelly says that he finds it 'not unreasonable' to

---

[9]   Donnelly, 'Eschatological Enquiry', p. 27.
[10] Donnelly, 'Eschatological Enquiry', p. 30.

believe that God, 'consistent with his unswerving respect for
human freedom', would give the inhabitants of heaven glorified
bodies free of physical impediment. He immediately adds that
sin would still be possible in heaven, saying that to forget this
would be to ignore the 'crucial lesson' of the fallen angels.[11] He
agrees that those in heaven will be made 'like angels', but holds
that angels themselves are not 'programmed' by God to be good
but have to face 'challenges' and 'opportunities' in heaven.[12]
The moral of the story of the angelic fall is that it is possible to
sin in heaven and so fall from there. Moreover, no human being
whom God is ready to admit to heaven would want to be
programmed to be happy at the cost of losing free will; and an
altogether benevolent God would not so fetter them. Such a
programmed angelic being would be a mere 'addict', rather
than an active agent of its own destiny, and its pleasures would
not be the achievements or fulfilments of a responsible person.[13]

   In responding to Wall's arguments, Donnelly seems to have
given up what are normally taken to be essential elements of
the notion of heaven: that it lasts forever and that its inhabitants
are unable to leave it. Heaven is normally conceived as a final
goal and resting-place, a permanent homeland to which those
who seek it journey through this present life. Donnelly refuses
to take this view, allowing instead that heaven may *not* be the
final destination of any individual, and that the journey of any
individual can involve both leaving and re-entering heaven any
number of times. Richard Swinburne can be cited as an example
of a philosopher of religion who conceives of heaven along more
conventional lines as a final resting-place. As recently as 1998
he has written that on earth human beings have the 'great good
of free and efficacious choice', and this allows him to deal in
part with the problem of evil by the kind of 'free will defence'
scorned by Wall: if human beings are to have this good, then
sin is 'virtually inevitable'. So it is good, Swinburne holds, for
free agents to have the choice in this world of finally rejecting
the good, though this is not what God seeks for them. What
God seeks is to take human beings to himself in a 'marvellous'

[11]   Donnelly, 'Eschatological Enquiry', p. 22.
[12]   Donnelly, 'Eschatological Enquiry', pp. 22–3.
[13]   Donnelly, 'Eschatological Enquiry', p. 23.

heavenly world which yet lacks 'a few goods which our world contains, including the good of being able to choose to reject the good'. Swinburne emphasises that a vast range of possible goods *is* available for choice in heaven, but excludes from it certain goods, including the good of being able to reject the good and depart.[14] Wall and Donnelly, however, would reject any such attempt to maintain freedom while excluding so crucial a choice. From their perspective, Swinburne's heaven or any which excluded the possibility of this crucial choice would not be truly free.

So both Wall and Donnelly take an exclusion of sin from heaven to entail the exclusion of freedom. While they are opposed on the ultimate worth of the concept of heaven, both share a common view on the value of human freedom. While Wall supposes the Christian concept of heaven to be discredited because it excludes freedom through its exclusion of sin, Donnelly maintains that the orthodox concept of heaven includes freedom and therefore the real possibility of sin. Neither supposes that the freedom of the blessed and their impeccability are in any way compatible. At least on the surface, there appears to be a tension in the Christian notion of heaven between freedom on the one hand and impeccability on the other. Donnelly, however, has made the suggestion against Wall that impeccability does not belong to the heaven of orthodox Christianity at all. Before we proceed further, we must first put this claim to the test, and then go on to say something of the notion of freedom operative in the work of Wall and Donnelly.

If the question of the impeccability and freedom of the blessed has been so little addressed by philosophers and theologians in recent times, that has also been true of most of Christian history. The Christians of the early Church believed in the eternity of heaven and the sinlessness of its members, but rarely asked whether heaven's inhabitants had the power to sin or depart from there. At the very least it was assumed that the blessed are de facto sinless, even if the possibility of their inability to sin is not raised. Some Fathers of the Church go further and see

[14] R. Swinburne, *Providence and the Problem of Evil* (Oxford: Clarendon Press, 1998), pp. 250–1. See also *Responsibility and Atonement* (Oxford: Clarendon Press, 1989), p. 190.

sin as no longer even a possibility for the blessed on account of the Spirit's gift of immutability, sin being possible only in a mutable being.[15] It was Augustine, however, who developed further the notion of heavenly impeccability and first explicitly raised the question of the relationship between this notion and human freedom.

The background to Augustine's crucial contribution lies in the thought of the third-century Alexandrian theologian, Origen. Origen's eschatology was controversial – it suggested the restoration of all rational creatures, the devil included – but so was his 'protology'. Origen thought that pre-existent souls had fallen from the contemplation of God into a bodily life on earth. Their restoration consisted in their return to divine contemplation. Indeed Origen held the principle that 'the end is always like the beginning'.[16] So although he seems to have taken this restoration to be a permanent one, his critics took him to be teaching that future falls were possible: if souls had once fallen from this state they could so fall again.[17] Although the evidence on whether or not Origen took heaven to be a truly final state is conflicting, there were among his followers those who explicitly endorsed a cyclical universe. What is at stake then is not simply the pre-existence of souls. Even if we discount this view (and indeed it was rejected by Origen's fellow Christians, Augustine included), there is still the question of what difference there might or might not be between the state of human beings at the 'beginning' and their state at the 'end'. While Origen seems to have supposed the final state to be a higher one, his critics thought that these states had to be distinguished with much greater precision or else there would be no final victory over evil and the history of the universe would be one of constant falls from heaven and subsequent restorations. If we discount the universal and cosmic dimension, this 'Origenist' account is not too far removed from the views

---

[15] See B. E. Daley SJ, *The Hope of the Early Church: A Handbook of Patristic Eschatology* (Cambridge: Cambridge University Press, 1991), pp. 112, 115.

[16] *De Principiis*, 1.6.2; 3.6.1 (GCS, vol. XXII, pp. 79–82, 279–82; ET: G. Butterworth, *On First Principles*; Gloucester, MA: Peter Smith, 1973, pp. 53–6, 245–7).

[17] See Daley, *Hope of the Early Church*, p. 237, n. 28.

of heaven proposed centuries later by Wall and Donnelly: the heavenly inhabitant can always 'slip out' and slip back in.

On Augustine's account there is a clear difference between a rational creature in its pre-fall state and a rational creature at its heavenly fulfilment.[18] Before their fall, both angels and the first human beings were able not to sin but were also able to sin. They could either sin or not sin. In the beatific vision, however, both angels and human beings are unable to sin. Sin is no longer a possibility for them, as it was in the beginning. While in the beginning they were only able not to sin, to avoid sin, at the end they are simply unable to sin at all. The same distinctions are made for human beings in the matter of death. At the beginning human beings were able not to die and able to die, but at the end they are simply unable to die. Being able not to die and able to die goes with being able not to sin and able to sin, and being unable to die goes with being unable to sin. These two states are of course not the only ones: between the state of justice or rectitude in which the first human beings were created and the state of heavenly glory, there lie the state of the fallen sinner and the one who has been justified by divine grace. The sinner is enslaved to sin and unable to persist in the good. The sinner is freed from this slavery by divine grace: by grace the justified are able once more not to sin as well as to sin, though they still must die. It is on account of this same divine grace that the justified are able to merit and so after death be rewarded by God with heaven, in which they are no longer able to sin or to die.[19]

This scheme then solves some of the problems thrown up by the so-called Origenist scheme. The difference between the initial state and the end state is now much clearer. There is now no possibility of a succession of falls and restorations, because it is impossible to fall from the end-state in which one is unable to sin. It was only possible to fall from the first state, in which sin was a possibility in addition to not sinning. It can be seen

[18] *De Civitate Dei*, bk 11, chs 11 and 12 (CCSL XLVIII, pp. 332–3; ET: J. O'Meara, *Concerning the City of God Against the Pagans*; London: Penguin, 1967, pp. 442–4).
[19] *De Civitate Dei*, bk 22, ch. 30 (CCSL XLVIII, pp. 863–4; ET: J. O'Meara, *Concerning the City of God Against the Pagans*; London: Penguin, 1967, pp. 1088–9).

immediately how the Augustinian scheme also differs from Donnelly's. Donnelly bases the orthodoxy of his view of heaven, namely that one can sin in heaven, on the supposition that the devil sinned in, and so fell from, heaven. But on the Augustinian view, the devil fell not from the full reality of heaven, but from a probationary state in which he was able not to sin and able to sin. Had the devil been created in the full reality of heaven, he would have been unable to sin. But he was not. So if we distinguish that state from which the devil fell from the final state of heaven, that makes it difficult for Donnelly to maintain the orthodoxy of his own notion of heaven.

It was in fact Augustine's view on impeccability which emerged as the orthodox Christian view, making Wall quite right in supposing the orthodox view of heaven to exclude the possibility of moral evil. Naturally enough the Fathers after Augustine taught the exclusion of sin from heaven just as they had done before Augustine. Heavenly impeccability is preached, and impeccability is understood to be a necessary part of beatitude: if one knew one could lose beatitude one would simply never be happy.[20] The medieval theologians followed in the tradition of Augustine, drawing on what he has to say in the *City of God* and elsewhere. Important textbooks of theology such as Peter Lombard's *Sentences* follow Augustine's distinctions and take it as established fact that the blessed cannot sin.[21]

Much medieval theology in the university was done as commentary not only on the Bible but also on Peter Lombard's *Sentences*. Heavenly impeccability proved to win a full consensus among the schoolmen. Where they differed was on how to *explain* impeccability, and different theories of impeccability arose, as we shall see in subsequent chapters. In later medieval times, it became more commonly asked whether God by his absolute power could have ordained a heavenly world in which sin was possible, but it was always taken that this was not the heavenly world that God had in fact ordained.

[20] See Daley, *Hope of the Early Church*, pp. 206, 208.
[21] *Sententiae in IV Libris Distinctae*, bk 2, dist. 25, c. 6 (Grottaferrata: Ad Claras Aquas, 1971, vol. I, pp. 464–5).

That impeccability belongs to the orthodox Christian concept of heaven is thus beyond any doubt. It emerged in patristic and medieval times as the consensus position and it did not become a bone of contention at the Protestant Reformation. The 'eternity' or 'perpetuity' of heaven was taken to be a matter of faith, and impeccability was an aspect of how theologians explained the fact that heaven could never be lost and so remained for ever. It must be added that Donnelly's notion of purgatory and what is implicit in it concerning death and the particular judgement would also hardly pass for Catholic orthodoxy, but I want to leave those matters on one side and pass on now to the notion of freedom.

As will become clear in the course of the following chapters, the notion of freedom is not straightforward, but only deceptively so. Philosophers have, however, debated the problem of freedom and determinism for centuries. The fact that human beings are held to be morally responsible for their actions has always been used as an argument for their actions being free rather than determined. This link between freedom and morality can immediately be recognised in Donnelly's desire to maintain freedom in heaven, so that the latter will be a realm of moral responsibility: without freedom there can be no morality.[22] The notion of human freedom has, however, from time to time suffered attack by advocates of 'determinism'. There is, nevertheless, a contemporary movement, with historical antecedents and known as 'compatibilism', that holds that freedom and determinism are in fact consistent. Such a movement is of course bound to be held by others who advocate freedom as a betrayal of freedom. Among those who think freedom and determinism incompatible, there are both those who are thoroughgoing determinists and those who champion freedom, and Wall and Donnelly would seem to fall into the second category. Such philosophers are known as 'libertarians'. They maintain human freedom and responsibility for present and future actions which have not been determined by the events of the past. Human agents can thus be causes of events without themselves being determined.

[22] Donnelly, 'Eschatological Enquiry', pp. 27, 30.

Not only the power to act but also the opportunity to act are often held to be essential to freedom. Freedom is normally analysed in terms of both an absence of determining influences and the fact that acts proceed from a human being as his or her own acts. Although there is no universal agreement on exactly how to define freedom, of immense influence is the 'freedom of indifference': what is crucial to human freedom is not simply that a course of action be the one the agent desires and causes without being determined to do so, but that the agent has chosen it from among alternative courses of action. Freedom of will comes down to choice, and the freedom of indifference means that each course of action is a genuine possibility for the will's choice. Since courses of action which are morally reprehensible are evidently open to human choice, advocates of the freedom of indifference may naturally suppose the freedom to do ill to be of the very essence of the notion of freedom. Indeed the fact that people freely do what they know to be wrong is partly what makes free will such an interesting avenue of enquiry for moral philosophers. Again, one can see the notion of freedom for contraries at work in the articles by Wall and Donnelly.[23] However, I have also noted some philosophers who raise the possibility of a world in which all choices are good ones. Nevertheless, such suggestions are made only in particular contexts, such as objections to the free will defence of God's allowing evil. In general, it is presupposed that free will means the freedom to do wrong as well as right. Hence the real meaning of Liddle's question of the existence of free will in heaven concerned the possibility of sin in heaven. But if the inhabitants of heaven turn out to be impeccable, they would appear to be unfree. With such a tension then between impeccability and free will, it would come as no surprise if so great a theologian as St Thomas Aquinas were to be reputed to deny freedom to the blessed on account of their impeccability. And one author has indeed recently asserted: 'Aquinas is happy to concede that we will not be free in heaven.'[24]

[23]   See above.
[24]   R. Cross, *Duns Scotus* (New York and Oxford: Oxford University Press, 1999), p. 150.

Such then is the problem of the freedom and impeccability of the blessed. I hope to seek an answer to this problem in the following pages by way of an analysis of the contributions of various distinguished theologians of the past. We shall begin with a theologian who stands at the beginning of the modern period and the close of medieval times, one whose doctrine can help us understand how more extreme positions such as those of Wall and Donnelly have arisen, before delving back into the teachings of his medieval predecessors.

2

Freedom, Necessity
and the Voluntary:
Francisco Suárez

Why moderns like Donnelly should be concerned with the
question of freedom and impeccability in heaven, a question in
fact treated in most detail by medieval thinkers, can be
illustrated by a scholastic thinker who stood both at the end of
medieval scholasticism and at the beginning of modern philosophy and theology. This scholastic was the Spanish Jesuit,
Francisco Suárez (1548–1617). Suárez drew not only on the
different strands of medieval thought, for example attempting
to mediate between Thomas Aquinas and Duns Scotus, but also
made use of fresh modes of presentation in philosophy suited
to his own time. His metaphysics exercised significant influence
on nascent modern philosophy, and his works were put to use
in Protestant as well as Catholic institutions. He was without
doubt the most important theologian of the Society of Jesus,
and the originator of a very influential way of interpreting St
Thomas and other scholastics in a modern setting. His influence
was particularly felt in moral theology, then gaining ground as
a discipline distinct from dogmatic theology, in which he
brought the notions of command and obligation to the fore.

Suárez directly addresses the issue of impeccability in the
beatific vision in his treatise on the 'end' of human beings, *De
Fine Hominis*. This posthumously published treatise consists of
sixteen disputations arising from St Thomas's *Summa Theologiae*,
on which Suárez was commenting. The tenth of these disputations includes the question whether heavenly 'beatitude' (or
'happiness') confirms the will of the blessed in the good, such
that they are made unable to sin. It is in the course of treating

15

this question that Suárez asks whether the blessed are free as well as impeccable. As for the main question, Suárez has no difficulty in reaching the conclusion that the blessed can neither sin and remain in beatitude, nor sin and thereby lose their beatitude. It is an error contrary to the latter position that Suárez attributes to Origen, an error that denies the perpetuity and security of beatitude. While Origen is said to have thought that the blessed could sin and thereby lose their beatitude, in fact they cannot. The blessed cannot sin at all.[1]

However, while Suárez has no difficulty in establishing the *fact* of the impeccability of the blessed, he admits that the 'special difficulty' of the question lies in determining the *cause and mode* of this impeccability. Are we concerned here with something intrinsic or something altogether extrinsic? Suárez gives it as the opinion of 'many' theologians, Scotus and William of Ockham among them, that the blessed are impeccable not by dint of the vision of God itself, but rather through divine providence alone. In other words, they are impeccable not by way of any intrinsic cause but by way of one that was altogether *extrinsic*.[2] I shall return to the latter theory in the next chapter.

Suárez's preferred opinion – what he calls the 'truer' one – is that the blessed are rendered *intrinsically* impeccable by way of beatitude itself, that is, by those very acts which themselves render a human being essentially blessed. While Thomas Aquinas had identified beatitude with the intellect's act of vision and Duns Scotus had identified it with the will's act of charity, Suárez sees acts of both will and intellect as essentially involved in beatitude, though he associates impeccability more closely with vision, as we shall see. And just as with the extrinsic theory, Suárez associates the intrinsic theory with a range of theologians, this time including St Thomas and many of the latter's disciples (Thomists). The argument itself is based on the vision of God as the most perfect beatitude. As such this beatitude has the greatest necessary perfection, rendering the blessed immutable in the good, unchangeable in their 'rectitude of will' (*rectitudine voluntatis*). What remains to be determined, however,

---

[1]   *De Fine Hominis*, disp. 10, sect. 1, nn. 1–3 (*Opera Omnia*, vol. IV, pp. 116–17).
[2]   *De Fine Hominis*, disp. 10, sect. 1, n. 4 (IV, p. 117).

is precisely *how* the 'free will' (*liberum arbitrium*) – which is by nature mutable – is prevented by the beatific vision from inclining to sin. What is it about the beatific vision that makes it intrinsically affect the will in this way?[3]

One possible explanation Suárez attributes to Durandus, a fourteenth-century Dominican who was important in the debates of his own time concerning the beatific vision, but Suárez also finds hints at this argument in Thomas's *Summa Contra Gentiles*.[4] The explanation takes its cue from the idea that the blessed see in the vision of God all the things and actions that pertain to them. Now given the Aristotelian principle that one cannot sin unless there is already a defect of some kind in the intellect, full knowledge of all that pertains to one should exclude the possibility of sin.[5] Suárez, however, is disinclined to embrace this explanation for impeccability. First of all, he is uncertain about the principle that sin must *always* presuppose defect of knowledge, thinking that difficult to *prove*. He agrees that there is never sin without such a defect *as a rule*. Consequently he is prepared to say that the full knowledge in question would give rise to a kind of *moral* impeccability: it would be morally impossible for there to be sin without some defect presupposed in the intellect. However, in connection with the beatific vision, Suárez wants to prove not a merely moral impeccability but an *absolute* impeccability, in which sin is excluded not merely as a rule but absolutely.[6]

Suárez's second difficulty with this explanation is uncertainty as to the extent of what is in fact seen by the blessed in the essence of God. He thinks that there are doubts about how much of what concerns one *is* seen in the beatific vision of God after all. But even granted that they do see such things, Suárez does not want to base impeccability on the vision of anything other

---

[3]   *De Fine Hominis*, disp. 10, sect. 1, n. 5 (IV, p. 117).

[4]   *Summa Contra Gentiles*, bk 4, ch. 92 (Leonine, vol. XV, p. 288; ET: C. J. O'Neil, *On the Truth of the Catholic Faith. Summa Contra Gentiles*; Garden City, NY: Hanover House, 1957, vol. 4, p. 340).

[5]   *De Fine Hominis*, disp. 10, sect. 1, n. 6 (IV, p. 117). Cf. Aristotle, *Nicomachean Ethics*, bk 3, ch. 1 (1110b 28–30; ET: H. Rackham, with text, in vol. 19 of the Loeb rev. edn of Aristotle; Cambridge, MA: Harvard University Press/London: Heinemann, 1934, pp. 120–1).

[6]   *De Fine Hominis*, disp. 10, sect. 1, n. 7 (IV, p. 117).

than *God himself*, even on things that are seen in God. Suárez does not want to make the vision of God himself, the very essence of goodness, insufficient for impeccability, and this he would do, he thinks, if he appealed to the vision of anything beyond God himself as necessary for impeccability. It is the vision of *God himself* that beatifies, not the vision of other things in God, so it should be the vision of *God himself* and not of things in God that renders the blessed impeccable. This, he thinks, is also truer to the general thought of St Thomas.[7]

Suárez next gives some lengthy consideration to the idea that the beatific vision renders the will impeccable *only indirectly*.[8] It would then be the act of charity that would render the will impeccable, such that the act of vision does so only by way of charity's mediating function. In the previous disputation on the perfection of the will with regard to God, Suárez had already argued his position that, given the fact of the vision of God, an act of perfect love of God, of charity, is *necessitated*. Someone with a clear vision of God could not but see that God is the supreme good, supremely loveable, the source of all goodness, and the end of all things. Consequently, the vision of God is sufficient to necessitate love of him: one cannot see the goodness of God and not love him. In adhering to this opinion Suárez was in the company of the Thomist school, though while the Thomists attributed this position to St Thomas, Suárez himself had doubts whether it was in fact Thomas's opinion. But whatever was the case with Thomas himself, Suárez and the Thomist school agreed that the beatific vision necessitated an act of charity.[9]

I should add here that, on this theory, love is necessary both in terms of the exercise of this act (*quoad exercitium*) and also in terms of its 'species' or specification (*quoad specificationem*).[10] Another example should make clear the distinction between the two kinds of necessity. The distinction figures again in the question as to whether the blessed love their own (created) beatitude. The question here is not about their love of *God* but

7   *De Fine Hominis*, disp. 10, sect. 1, nn. 7–8 (IV, p. 118).
8   *De Fine Hominis*, disp. 10, sect. 1, nn. 9–15 (IV, pp. 118–20).
9   *De Fine Hominis*, disp. 9, sect. 1 (IV, pp. 104–10).
10 *De Fine Hominis*, disp. 9, sect. 1, n. 20 (IV, p. 109).

their love of their own *happiness* or beatitude in loving him. Suárez's answer is that they love it necessarily in terms of specification, but do *not* love it necessarily in terms of exercise.[11] In other words, they cannot hate their own beatitude (it is loved necessarily *quoad specificationem*), but they are not required always to be exercising an act of loving it (their beatitude is not loved necessarily *quoad exercitium*). While they need not always be actually loving their beatitude, they cannot go against it and hate it. However, in the case of the beatific love of *God*, the act is necessary in both senses. The fact that it is necessary in the sense of specification can be deduced from the fact that it is necessary in the sense of exercise: if one must always be exercising this love one can never will against it. Suárez argues moreover that a perfect friendship, such as is had with God, must involve a conformity of wills. Consequently, one who has such a love for the end to which all things must be referred, conforms his will to the divine will, and without this conformity his love could not be stable. The necessity of specification has to do with this conformity of the will to God's will.[12] So while loving *God* is necessary in terms of exercising this act, the love of one's beatitude in heaven is *not* necessary in terms of exercising the act. The love of *God* is necessary, however, both in terms of its specification *and* in terms of its exercise. The blessed cannot hate God, and must *always* be exercising their love of him, given that they see his goodness face to face.

Taking these presuppositions into a theory of charity as the intrinsic cause of impeccability, one would conclude that the vision of God necessitates an act of love of him, which would in turn itself necessitate impeccability: such a perfect love would see that everything done would be referred to God as ultimate end, such that one would never act contrary to that end. In other words, the act of loving God in heaven rules out the possibility of sin. Though support can be found for this way of speaking not only in Thomas and his disciples but also in the Fathers,[13] Suárez prefers to say that it is the vision itself rather

---

[11] *De Fine Hominis*, disp. 9, sect. 2 (IV, p. 110–12).
[12] *De Fine Hominis*, disp. 9, sect. 1, n. 20 (IV, p. 109).
[13] *De Fine Hominis*, disp. 10, sect. 1, n. 10 (IV, p. 118).

than the love it necessitates which is responsible for impeccability. This is the approach he finds in the sixteenth-century Dominican, Cardinal Cajetan, and Suárez agrees that it best represents the mind of St Thomas. Suárez imagines someone engaged in the contemplation of God, considering his goodness and judging that all things should be referred to this divine goodness. Such a person could scarcely sin, Suárez says, without first ceasing from contemplation. As long as one is engaged in such contemplation, one could hardly engage at the very same time in sin.

How much more, Suárez says, will this apply in the beatific vision, an act from which one can never cease. There the object clearly seen will of itself necessitate the will to exercise an act of love of it. Suárez takes the view that *if* the latter act of *charity* is itself made the cause of impeccability, it would follow that, if God by his absolute power were to cease to hold that act of charity in existence, then the act of *vision*, not itself being the cause of impeccability, would be *insufficient* to keep the soul impeccable. The implication would be that a soul seeing God but somehow not actually engaged in loving him would be able to sin. However, Suárez refuses to think that that would be the case. He holds instead that if God were indeed by his absolute power to cease to hold the act of charity in existence, then the act of vision of God would still be sufficient that the will be inclined to its object by its natural impulse and by (the habit or virtue of) charity. So even if charity's necessity of exercise had been suspended by God's absolute power, the necessity of specification would remain. Even though such a soul would no longer be engaged in a necessary act of loving God, it would necessarily be unable to will anything contrary to the divine goodness which it saw, and whatever acts it did will would be done either with respect to the divine goodness itself or would be referred to that goodness. On this account, it is the act of *seeing* God rather than the act of love of him which would be the intrinsic cause of impeccability.

Suárez then draws on St Thomas: God must be sufficient for the one who sees him, or else the vision of God would not make this soul truly blessed. So, if seeing God *does* make him truly blessed, then God must be sufficient for him. Consequently, the blessed one will not will anything else that is not in God or that is not referred to him.[14] Suárez holds, moreover, that through the act of vision God and his goodness are seen such that this object is preferred to all things, and the will is turned to nothing that is not in conformity with this goodness. The act of vision of this goodness is so efficacious as to turn the whole soul to it, so that those who see him can never will anything that has not first been measured against the divine goodness to see that it is in conformity with it.[15]

It is part of Suárez's theory that the blessed *necessarily* do what they judge to have a necessary connection with the divine goodness. Indeed necessity is a prominent feature throughout Suárez's account of the beatific vision: the soul that sees God is *necessitated* by that very act of vision to exercise love of him. However, freedom was also important to Suárez's agenda both in terms of moral theology and in terms of controversies with both Protestant denials of freedom and Dominican views on the relationship between human freedom and divine grace. So, given the predominance of necessity in Suárez's theology of beatitude, it is not surprising that, after setting out his views on heavenly impeccability, Suárez should ask whether there is still freedom in the beatific vision, despite this inability to sin. This Suárez presents as 'that difficult question': How does 'freedom' (*libertas*) remain in the blessed? Characteristically, he is especially concerned with how freedom remains with respect to acts which have been *commanded*, particularly in view of the fact that the act of loving God is necessary. He notes that the whole question had been addressed by Anselm in his *De Libertate Arbitrii* and by Augustine in the *Enchiridion* and in the *City of God*.[16] Suárez gives no extended treatment of what they have to say, and goes on to dismiss them quite briefly. Nevertheless, I shall take this opportunity of giving some

[14]   *De Fine Hominis*, disp. 10, sect. 1, n. 16 (IV, p. 120), citing *Summa Contra Gentiles*, bk 4, ch. 92 (XV, p. 288; ET: vol. 4, p. 340).
[15]   *De Fine Hominis*, disp. 10, sect. 1, n. 17 (IV, p. 120).
[16]   *De Fine Hominis*, disp. 10, sect. 1, n. 20 (IV, p. 121). The passage from the *Enchiridion* is ch. 28, n. 105 (CCSL XLVI, p. 106; ET: Bernard M. Peebles in vol. 4 of *Writings of Saint Augustine* in *The Fathers of the Church. A New Translation*; New York: Cima, 1947, pp. 458–9).

account of what Augustine and Anselm were saying in these books.[17]

The passage from the *City of God* I have already referred to in Chapter 1. Augustine was distinguishing the pre-fall state of Adam and Eve as allowing the possibility to sin and not to sin, to die and not to die, from the final state of heaven, where one was unable to sin and unable to die. In the same passage Augustine states of the blessed: 'Now the fact that they will not be able to delight in sin does not entail that they have no free will.'[18] That he makes such a confident statement at all reveals that Augustine at least understands that ours is a genuine question that someone might raise: Does the heavenly inability to sin exclude freedom of choice on the part of the blessed? So Augustine at least understands that someone might think that *liberum arbitrium* was excluded by the exclusion of the ability to sin, and that this mistaken thought ought to have a response.

He counters with the assertion that the will will in fact be *freer* in heaven. He speaks of the blessed having been freed from delight in sinning for a delight in not sinning. From this delight in not sinning they cannot turn away: it is *indeclinabilem*.[19] They have been moved from the state of sin to the state of heavenly glory and impeccability. There appear to be two aspects to this greater freedom: a comparison with the state from which it has emerged, and the character of the state in which it exists in heaven. So the first point is that the last state of free will will be more powerful than the state of delight in sin, if only because, as Augustine says, the free will had to be *freed* from that sinful state. To be freed from slavery is obviously to receive a greater freedom of will than whatever such freedom one had before. The second aspect is the 'indeclinability' of the freed will in

---

[17] Augustine's views on freedom have normally been discussed in connection with his teaching on grace, on which there is a great deal of literature. More recent discussion on both figures has raised the question of whether or not their views on the freedom of non-beatified rational creatures were libertarian or compatibilist. See, e.g., K. A. Rogers, *The Anselmian Approach to God and Creation* (Lampeter: Edward Mellen Press, 1997), pp. 91–101, and *The Neoplatonic Metaphysics and Epistemology of Anselm of Canterbury* (Lampeter: Edward Mellen Press, 1997), esp. pp. 82–5.

[18] *De Civitate Dei*, bk 32, ch. 30 (p. 863; ET: p. 1089).

[19] *De Civitate Dei*, bk 32, ch. 30 (p. 863; ET: p. 1089).

heaven: this very indeclinability is taken to *make* it freer. In other words, the suggestion that impeccability entails lack of free will is countered by the assertion that impeccability in fact entails a greater free will, presumably because one is permanently free of sin and unhappiness: subsequent theology would often speak of freedom from sin in this life and freedom from misery in the next.

So far Augustine has explicitly spoken only of heavenly impeccability being a freer state than that from which the sinner needs to be freed. He has not explicitly spoken of heavenly impeccability being greater than the state of the justified intermediate between sinfulness and heaven, a state in which one is able not to sin and able to sin, a state thus comparable to the original state in which the first human beings were constituted. This is remedied however by Augustine's very next assertion concerning that first state: 'For the first free will, given to man when he was created righteous, consisted in an ability not to sin and an ability to sin; but the final free will will be more potent, because it will consist in not being able to sin.'[20] The greater freedom of heaven in comparison to all the other historical states of human freedom is now clearly asserted. Moreover, it is given an explanation identical to the second aspect of the explanation already given: it is precisely on account of its impeccability (and hence permanent freedom from sin and unhappiness) that heavenly free will is more powerful.

Augustine next goes on to make an important qualification of heavenly impeccability, distinguishing it carefully from divine impeccability. Heavenly impeccability is a gift of grace and not something of nature. It is one thing, Augustine says, to be God and another to participate in God. God is of course impeccable by nature, but one who participates in God is not impeccable by nature but receives impeccability from God as a gift.[21] Augustine's next point is that the different grades of free will were given by God in accordance with his plan. In this plan God wanted to enable human beings to merit the reward of heaven. So first he gives them the conditions for meriting,

[20] *De Civitate Dei*, bk 32, ch. 30 (p. 863; ET: p. 1089).
[21] *De Civitate Dei*, bk 32, ch. 30 (p. 863; ET: p. 1089).

and then in response to their merit gives them their reward. The first gift is the free will appropriate to one who has to acquire merit, while the final gift pertains to the reward. Thus the initial free will is the ability not to sin and the ability to sin (pertaining to acquisition of merit), and the final free will is the inability to sin (pertaining to reception of the reward). Augustine then adds that since human nature made use of the ability to sin, it is a more abundant gift of grace that sets it free so that it might be brought to that freedom in which sin was impossible. This allusion to Adam's sin leads to a comparison between the initial and final states in respect of freedom and sin on the one hand and those same states in respect of death and immortality on the other. There is here a clear parallel: as the first immortality was the ability not to die (an ability lost by Adam's sin) and the last immortality the inability to die, the first free will was the ability not to sin and the last the inability to sin.[22]

Augustine now attempts to explain the inability to sin a little further:

> Sic enim erit inamissibilis voluntas pietatis et aequitatis, quo modo est felicitatis. Nam utique peccando nec pietatem nec felicitatem tenuimus, voluntatem vero felicitatis nec perdita felicitate perdidimus.

> For the will to piety and equity will then not be able to be lost, just as the will to happiness cannot now be lost. For by sinning we held on to neither piety nor happiness, but we did not lose the will to happiness when we lost happiness.[23]

The argument is that impeccability is explained by the fact that in heaven one will not be able to lose the will to piety and equity. This inability is in turn illustrated by the fact that in this present life we cannot lose the will to happiness. Augustine reminds his readers that sin has in fact lost us both happiness and piety, but the will to happiness has itself not been extinguished. Augustine wants to say that just as we cannot ever lose the will for happiness here on earth, the will for piety and equity will

---

[22] *De Civitate Dei*, bk 32, ch. 30 (pp. 863–4; ET: p. 1089).
[23] *De Civitate Dei*, bk 32, ch. 30 (p. 864; ET: p. 1089).

not be able to be lost in heaven. Trained as one is on piety and equity, one's will cannot turn away from its delight in not sinning.

Augustine focuses again explicitly on free will immediately after his account of the will for piety and equity, when he states, 'Certainly God himself cannot sin: can we therefore say that God has no free will?'[24] Augustine does not draw out the implication of this question: it is clear enough. Augustine assumes that everyone will agree with him in holding both that God has free will and that God cannot sin. It follows then from the fact that God is both free and impeccable that divine impeccability does not rule out divine freedom. No doubt then the same is true in the case of the blessed: their impeccability does not rule out their freedom. Augustine could have attempted more explicit argument here: he might have argued that heavenly freedom is more potent because it more nearly approaches the impeccable freedom of God, and that God's freedom must be the most perfect of all. He might also have attempted further argument as to why this heavenly impeccability entails freedom and the greatest of human freedoms. But he does no more at the end of this passage than establish from the case of the divine nature that freedom and impeccability are not mutually exclusive but can in fact go together. He concludes simply that there will be free will in heaven, adding that it will be the same freedom in all, indivisible in each heavenly inhabitant.

St Anselm was a monk of Bec at the end of the eleventh century, who not only became abbot but went on to become archbishop of Canterbury. From our perspective he was a medieval man, a transitional figure between the new age of scholasticism and earlier times. Despite this lack of antiquity, it seems that for Suárez he possessed the authority of a Church Father. Almost immediately after the opening of his *De Libertate Arbitrii*, Anselm rejects the suggestion that *liberum arbitrium* is the power to sin and not to sin. Since neither God nor the good angels can sin, and given that it would be impious to suggest they do not possess free will, free will cannot be the power to sin. For Anselm, the power to sin is neither freedom nor part of

---

[24]   *De Civitate Dei*, bk 32, ch. 30 (p. 864; ET: p. 1089).

freedom: in fact the power to sin diminishes freedom, and God and the blessed angels are freer than those able to sin.[25] Anselm therefore seeks out a different definition of freedom, one that can be applied to all rational beings, God included. He concludes that freedom of will is the power to preserve rectitude of will for its own sake.[26] Such free will remains in those who lose this rectitude, because although their rectitude is lost they have not lost the power to preserve it, just as people retain a power to see an object even when that object is absent.[27] For our purposes, we have only to note that, like God and the good angels, in the next life elect human beings possess this rectitude in such an inseparable way that it can never be lost.[28] In this way, they are more free than those who can lose it by sinning.

Suárez spends little time on these authorities: he simply represents their solutions as asserting that the blessed are in fact *more free* in that they are freer of sin. But to Suárez this just seems to be equivocation, and no doubt Wall and Donnelly would agree. Such 'freedom' is evidently different from what would seem to Suárez to be the proper sense of 'freedom', the freedom with which this question ought to be concerned. He would of course agree that the blessed are free from sin, but that is not the freedom at issue here, he thinks. Consequently he still wants to ask whether the blessed are free in what for him must be the *proper* sense of freedom.[29]

We shall return to an alternative approach to freedom in subsequent chapters, but for now, to fill out a little more what Suárez takes 'freedom' to mean, I turn to another treatise of his, *De Voluntario et Involuntario*. In the first disputation of the treatise, Suárez explores the relationship between the 'voluntary' and the 'free'.[30] There he states that the act of love in the beatific vision is an example of an act which is 'voluntary' – of the will – and yet is not free 'in the proper sense' (*in propria*

[25]   *De Libertate Arbitrii*, ch. 1 (*Opera Omnia*, I, pp. 207–9; ET: B. Davies and G. R. Evans, *The Major Works*; Oxford and New York: Oxford University Press, 1998, pp. 175–6).
[26]   *De Libertate Arbitrii*, ch. 3 (pp. 210–13; ET: pp. 178–80).
[27]   *De Libertate Arbitrii*, ch. 4 (pp. 213–14; ET: p. 181).
[28]   *De Libertate Arbitrii*, ch. 15 (p. 226; ET: p. 192).
[29]   *De Fine Hominis*, disp. 10, sect. 1, n. 20 (IV, p. 121).
[30]   *De Voluntario et Involuntario*, disp. 1, sect. 3, n. 10 (IV, p. 170).

significatione), but rather necessary. He concludes that 'freedom' does not belong to the notion of what is 'perfectly voluntary'. He also gives another example to prove his point: the act of love of God for himself by which the Holy Spirit proceeds from the Father and the Son. Such love is 'altogether necessary', he says, yet perfectly voluntary. Such acts are said to be voluntary because they proceed from perfect reason and knowledge and from a perfect will, such that what is perfectly voluntary cannot be lacking to them. Suárez holds that freedom does not always imply perfection, nor necessity imperfection. When a perfect will is related to an object which is excellent and known to be such, that will tends to the object in the most perfect way, that is, not freely but necessarily.[31]

So freedom is excluded from the most perfect acts of the will. Such acts could be called free only in the sense that they are free from external force or compulsion. Suárez allows freedom from compulsion to be truly predicated of something, however much it may otherwise be necessary. In this sense of freedom the blessed could be said to be free, however necessary their act of love is. This is only the first degree of freedom, however. Suárez names a further degree of freedom, which he says is a 'more perfect' freedom, namely, freedom not only from compulsion but also from simple necessity. This freedom is said to be more perfect because it excludes a greater subjection, making this a more generally accepted use of 'freedom'. A yet more perfect degree of freedom still is freedom not only from compulsion and absolute necessity, but also from necessity of weakness and bad habits. It was such a freedom in which the first human beings were constituted before the fall. This freedom enabled them to avoid sin, but they subsequently lost it through sin. Suárez's fourth and final degree of freedom is the exclusion not only of simple necessity, but also of obligation. It is on account of this crucial degree of freedom, he says, that one calls a law which is based on love rather than fear a 'law of freedom'.[32]

In his treatise *De Legibus et Legislatore Deo*, Suárez views law as something that proceeds from the will of the lawgiver and

---

[31] *De Voluntario et Involuntario*, disp. 1, sect. 3, n. 11 (IV, p. 170).
[32] *De Voluntario et Involuntario*, disp. 1, sect. 3, nn. 13–16 (IV, p. 171).

imposes obligation on the lawgiver's inferiors. Morality came to be seen primarily in terms of following the law, and Suárez sees law as the supreme norm of the rightness of action.[33] Suárez's moral theology was much concerned with the doubtful conscience, that is, what to do when a law did not oblige one to a particular action. A law that was doubtful was taken to impose no obligation, because, given the doubt that the law had 'possession' of one's conscience in such a case, it was *one's own freedom* that remained 'in possession' rather than the law. In his study of the Catholic tradition of moral theology, John Mahoney SJ notes that Suárez held a view of freedom as the 'great undetermined', with the will 'totally spontaneous to act and not to act'.[34] Suárez, he says, stresses individual moral freedom as what is primary, with morality as law requiring firm justification to encroach on this freedom. One's conscience and the law almost face each other as antagonists, with the individual judging whether or not his or her freedom should yield to the law. Mahoney's assessment leaves the impression that it was the limiting of the scope of law in various ways that enabled Suárez to carve out an area of free and unobliged human action, so important was it to him that there be a place for human freedom. When we turn back from this life to the next, we can discern something similar: the need to maintain an area of free, unobliged, unnecessitated human action in the beatific vision, in spite of the necessity with which the blessed love God and in spite of the exclusion of sin.

So, faced with the question of how freedom remains in the blessed, Suárez's *De Fine Hominis* answers by saying that they are no more free to obey a command than they are to love, or they are free in that they can act in various ways from various reasons and motives to fulfil what God has commanded. This scenario he takes as sufficient for their acts to be free. While they necessarily obey what God commands, they are free to act in various ways to fulfil his commands.[35] The matter is treated a little more fully, however, in Suárez's commentary on

[33] See J. Mahoney SJ, *The Making of Moral Theology: A Study of the Roman Catholic Tradition* (Oxford: Clarendon Press, 1987), pp. 226–8.
[34] Mahoney, *Making of Moral Theology*, pp. 228–9.
[35] *De Fine Hominis*, disp. 9, sect. 1, n. 20 (IV, p. 121).

the Third Part of St Thomas's *Summa Theologiae*. One of the questions which Suárez disputes concerns the meritorious nature of Christ's human acts. Suárez accepts that charity is the principle of merit and that Christ merited through acts of love for his neighbours. He also accepts that for an act to be meritorious, it must be free, entailing that Christ's meritorious acts of love for his neighbours had to be free.[36] This is a problem for Suárez, because he holds Christ to have possessed the beatific vision all through his life, implying that Christ loved his neighbours with beatific love, which was of course, on Suárez's view, necessary rather than free. So how could Christ have possibly merited by his charity, since the latter was necessary rather than free?[37]

Suárez considers the possibility – one favoured by the 'Thomists' – that the *same act* of charity could be necessary in regard to God but free in regard to contingent creatures, without any change to that act. While Suárez is willing to allow this of God's own act of charity, he is hardly willing to allow such a mystery to be applied to something created! His argument is *ad hominem*: If there are theologians who find difficulty in believing this of God's act of love, how will it be believed of a created act?[38] He is more open to the idea that the neighbour, even when seen in God, is not loved with the same beatific act by which God is loved, the latter act being of course necessary. On this view the blessed soul, although it sees neighbour in God, loves neighbour with a further but free act, God and neighbour each being loved by different acts of charity, the one necessary, the other free.[39] Suárez's own view, however, allows neighbour to be loved in both acts, one of which is again necessary with the other free. Christ's vision of God the Word and of neighbour in the Word necessitates an act in which God is primarily and directly loved and neighbour loved in him. That is the necessary

---

[36] *Commentary on the Third Part of the Summa Theologiae*, disp. 39, sect. 1, n. 3 (XVIII, p. 320).

[37] *Commentary on the Third Part of the Summa Theologiae*, disp. 39, sect. 2 (XVIII, pp. 325–30).

[38] *Commentary on the Third Part of the Summa Theologiae*, disp. 39, sect. 2, n. 9 (XVIII, pp. 327–8).

[39] *Commentary on the Third Part of the Summa Theologiae*, disp. 39, sect. 2, n. 10 (XVIII, p. 328).

act in which neighbour is loved in God who is himself directly loved. The other act of love of neighbour, namely, the free act, takes neighbour rather than God for its direct object, although God remains the reason for which the neighbour is loved though he is not loved directly. The two acts remain distinct, the one necessary (and more perfect) and the other free, and neither excludes the other. It is the second of these acts which, as free, becomes the basis of Christ's meriting.[40]

Though merit is not ascribed to the blessed in heaven, this reasoning does suggest a way in which free acts of love of neighbour might be ascribed to the blessed, just as (as we have already seen) the blessed are free in exercising love of their own (created) beatitude. Such acts are free, provided, of course, that they have not been *commanded*. This issue of commands arises in another of Suárez's difficulties, namely, how Christ can freely obey the command of the Father to undergo the passion. Suárez's problem is that if the passion were commanded by God, it would seem that Christ would necessarily obey that command, just as the blessed in heaven necessarily obey God's commands.[41] He is aware of various possible solutions – including the Thomist objection that one *can* of course obey God's commands *freely* – but he eventually deals with the problem by denying that the command to undergo the passion was a command in the strict sense of the term, thereby enabling Christ to be considered to go to the cross uncommanded and freely.[42]

As for what Suárez has to say of the blessed here, he again affirms that their beatific love of God is necessary, both with regard to the exercise of their act of love and with regard to its specification. So the blessed must love God actually and cannot will anything that is not referred to him. However, Suárez thinks that this does not mean that they must love him necessarily *in every way*. It is not necessary, he says, that the blessed always

[40] *Commentary on the Third Part of the Summa Theologiae*, disp. 39, sect. 2, nn. 10–13 (XVIII, pp. 328–9).

[41] *Commentary on the Third Part of the Summa Theologiae*, disp. 37, sect. 4 (XVIII, pp. 292–7).

[42] *Commentary on the Third Part of the Summa Theologiae*, disp. 37, sect. 4, n. 9 (XVIII, p. 296).

be exercising an act of willing God's honour or the extrinsic glory that comes to him through the conversion of human beings. These and other things of this kind are *secondary*, according to Suárez. It is true, he agrees, that when the blessed do will something concerning a secondary object, they will always act from perfect charity. However, it is not necessary that they always be making such acts. Nor, for the same reason, he says, is it necessary that in that act by which they necessarily love God, they should formally, explicitly and actually always be willing to fulfil the divine will in those things where there is neither a command nor any other obligation. Such matters are secondary and of absolute necessity neither to charity nor to beatitude. Consequently, no necessity with regard to exercise arises in such non-obligated acts. And so in respect of acts which are not commanded, all difficulties are said to cease. For such acts there is no obligation or necessity. They are done by the blessed in freedom.[43] It seems that Suárez has succeeded in finding an area of free action even in a heaven so seemingly dominated by necessity and the exclusion of sin. But how would this appear to Wall and Donnelly?

Suárez's theology of heavenly impeccability provides a good position from which to understand how a debate like the one between Wall and Donnelly could arise, and how Liddle could consider the question as to whether there will be free will in heaven to be so fascinating. Suárez's theology of heaven was, as we have seen, dominated by necessity, to which he opposed freedom. And when he declared that the soul's act of love was necessary rather than free, he was not expressing an isolated opinion, but what would be the consensus of much scholastic theology from the sixteenth to the twentieth century. Liddle's question arises from the suspicion that there will be no free will in heaven, because there we will be unable to sin. To some extent Suárez confirms this view: the vision of God, the act of seeing God, is responsible for the fact that one can no longer sin. Human freedom, at least in this respect, has been restricted. For Wall, such a view excludes human freedom altogether. For

---

[43] *Commentary on the Third Part of the Summa Theologiae*, disp. 37, sect. 4, n. 10 (XVIII, p. 296).

him, if the inhabitants in heaven cannot sin, then they cannot be free. Hence heaven cannot be attractive, because it excludes something human beings value highly, namely, their freedom. Donnelly, conceding much of Wall's position, but wanting to save heaven from its onslaught, reinvents heaven as a place where sin remains a possibility. However, he fails to demonstrate the Christian orthodoxy he claims for his view. We have seen that Suárez is not immune to their concern that freedom should not be jettisoned. Just as Suárez wanted to maintain a space for human freedom in the field of moral decision in the face of his emphasis on morality as following the law, so he wanted to maintain a space for human freedom in heaven in the face of an inescapable necessity and impeccability. Suárez's reasoning led him to affirm that freedom was not to be found in the most perfect of voluntary acts. However, he did not wish to abandon freedom altogether but found a place for it where the life of heaven brought neither necessity nor obligation.

Such a strategy, however, could hardly appeal to someone like Wall. There *is* a place for freedom in Suárez's account, but not the greater place that others might want to claim for it. Indeed Suárez's position is just the kind of theology against which opinions such as that of Wall arose, because it is the kind of theology of heaven that rules out something significant in the freedom we have on earth. Just as Mahoney discerns a tension, a confrontation, in Suárez's moral theology between freedom and obligation, so we have discerned an analogous tension in Suárez's eschatology between necessity and obligation on the one hand and freedom on the other. In the approach of Donnelly, freedom has overcome this tension but at the expense of impeccability. Donnelly was satisfied with his position, because in his view it secured not only freedom but also orthodoxy. But if the orthodox view is not Donnelly's but rather impeccability, then those who take Donnelly's position, if they continue to honour the value of orthodoxy, must embrace impeccability and modify their position on free will, though no doubt they would still want to grant freedom as great a value as possible in heaven and, if possible, a greater value than Suárez granted it in his kingdom of necessity.

The question now arises: Is it possible to construct a theology in which freedom is again accorded a greater value, but where the Christian orthodoxy of heavenly impeccability is retained, an orthodoxy that gives so great a place to freedom that someone like Donnelly might see the attraction of it and be won over? Of the thirteenth-century Franciscan friar, Duns Scotus, Robert P. Prentice waxes lyrical:

> Dialectically opposing himself to the necessitarianism espoused by a prior human consciousness, Scotus sees heaven as a vast kingdom of liberty in which man 'creates' himself by freely loving God, in which God freely conserves the ontological status of this free human 'creation', and in which God freely collaborates with man to make perpetually possible and actual the free psychological act of fruitional love which man directs to Himself.[44]

This suggests that Scotus not only gave freedom in heaven a greater value than Suárez accorded it, but that he also in some way maintained the impeccability of the blessed. So it is to Scotus that I turn in the next chapter.

---

[44] R. P. Prentice, 'The Degree and Mode of Liberty in the Beatitude of the Blessed', in *Deus et Homo ad mentem I. Duns Scoti* (Rome: Societas Internationalis Scotistica, 1972), p. 328.

3

Freedom, Infinite and Finite:
Duns Scotus

In the last chapter, we saw that Suárez took Scotus to hold the view that the blessed are impeccable only by way of extrinsic divine providence. To an extrinsic theory Suárez attributes two points. First, God would never concur with the blessed such that they might sin. Secondly, he would necessitate their love for him above all else such that they would never cease from this act of love. Both these would be by way of God's extrinsic providence rather than anything intrinsic to the blessed.[1]

Suárez goes on to give two possible accounts of this extrinsic theory. On the first account, the blessed would not be intrinsically necessitated to the vision of God. As a consequence, they would be able to cease from the beatific vision, and would then be able to sin once more. By his providence God would see to it that they never in fact ceased from the vision of God. For Suárez this view is in itself to be rejected because the vision itself is in fact necessary, and if the blessed were changeable so as to be able to lose the vision they would never have been truly blessed. The first account he says is more contrary to the *perpetuity* of the beatific vision than to impeccability, because one only becomes able to sin once one has ceased to be among the blessed. One ceases to be blessed by ceasing from the beatific vision, and only then does one regain one's peccability. So the blessed would be impeccable as long as they remained blessed, but they can cease to be blessed and *thenceforth* can sin. This, however, is not the view that Suárez

<hr>

[1]   *De Fine Hominis*, disp. 10, sect. 1, n. 4 (IV, p. 117).

attributes to Scotus and other proponents of the extrinsic theory, although it does in fact bear *some* resemblance to what Scotus says in an important respect, as we shall see.

The second account allows the blessed to retain the power to sin even while they see God, though God in fact prevents them from exercising this power by his providence. It is this version of the extrinsic theory that Suárez attributes to its proponents, Scotus included. The reasoning behind the theory is that the will of the blessed retains its ability to sin through the power of its own natural freedom. In other words, the will possesses its own natural freedom and is consequently able to sin, and the vision of God makes no difference to this fact. Given that there is nothing intrinsic that impedes this freedom or necessitates not sinning – neither knowledge nor love are thought by Scotus to be adequate to such tasks – it is only the extrinsic providence of God that prevents the blessed from committing actual sin. This second account then differs from the first in that on the second account the blessed can sin and thus lose their blessedness, while on the first account the blessed can only sin once they have ceased from the act by which they are blessed and have thus ceased to be blessed.

A more recent summary of Scotus's teaching has been given by Richard Cross, who devotes an appendix of his book on Scotus in the Great Medieval Thinkers Series to the beatific vision.[2] There he records that, according to Catholic teaching, the saints in heaven enjoy the beatific vision for ever, such that they cannot lose it. One way it might be lost would be through the saint's sin. Consequently, the saints in heaven must be impeccable. Cross presents the following as an 'obvious objection' to this teaching: if the saints cannot sin, it looks as though they cannot be free. It is here that Cross records his opinion – which I have already cited in Chapter 1 – that Aquinas concedes that the blessed are not free, and Cross would no doubt say the same of Suárez too. Cross says that Scotus rejects the view (attributed to Aquinas) that human beings cling to God necessarily when God shows himself directly to their wills, there being no possibility of an intellectual mistake in this case about

---

[2]   Cross, *Duns Scotus*, pp. 149–51.

the fact that God is what makes us truly happy. Scotus believed such a view, Cross says, to be 'profoundly mistaken', and his reason was the sort of thing he thought the human will to be. According to Scotus, the will always has the power to do other than it does. Changes in the will's external circumstances cannot change the way the will acts, not even being in the direct presence of God. According to Cross, Scotus's claim is that the will retains its power for refraining from eliciting an act of love for God in the beatific vision, even while it is in fact eliciting such an act.

Cross does not distinguish between two possible divergent accounts of the extrinsic theory, as Suárez does, but in his account of Scotus identifies refraining from an act of love for God in the beatific vision with a (sinful) failing to love God: 'the will retains its power for sinning (by failing to love God)'.[3] The fact that the will retains the power to refrain from actual love of God means that it retains the power for *sinning*, because to refrain from loving God (that is, to fail to love him) *is* a sin. Suárez distinguished two possible accounts of the extrinsic theory, one in which the blessed soul could refrain from loving God and then would be able to sin, and another (attributed to Scotus) in which the blessed soul always retained the power to sin. Cross, however, takes the refraining from the elicited act of love itself to be a sin. So, on Cross's account, Scotus would hold that the blessed retain the power to refrain from loving God, but the point is that such refraining would not simply open up the way to sin but would itself *be* a sin. The power to refrain from loving God is a power to sin. As we shall see, Cross has discerned the mind of Scotus correctly.

Cross continues his account of Scotus by saying that the will cannot use its power to sin (that is, refrain from the love of God) because it *lacks the opportunity* to do so. The blessed soul is prevented by a higher cause (namely, God) from willing the opposite, even though it retains the capacity to will the opposite. This claim of Scotus's leads Cross (as indeed it leads Scotus) to the objection of determinism.[4] On Scotus's theory, does not God

3   Cross, *Duns Scotus*, p. 150.
4   Cross, *Duns Scotus*, p. 150–1.

extrinsically *determine* the will, and so eliminate its freedom? It is in recounting Scotus's response to this objection that Cross claims Scotus for a compatibilist in the contemporary debate among philosophers as to whether or not freedom and determinism are compatible. In claiming him for a compatibilist, Cross touches lightly on a further scholarly debate as to the exact nature of Scotus's views on freedom.

While Scotus has normally been considered by scholars to be a 'voluntarist', helping to give rise to the modern notion of the will as undetermined, with freedom of indifference, freedom of choice, as central (in other words, a 'libertarian' and 'incompatibilist'), Douglas Langston has claimed that for Scotus such freedom between alternatives is in fact *compatible* with determinism, and Cross follows Langston.[5] Other scholars, however, such as William A. Frank, have argued for a quite different notion of freedom in Scotus's writings, one derived from St Anselm.[6] Joseph M. Incandela has claimed that there are *two* divergent notions of freedom sitting very uneasily together in Scotus's thought.[7] Frank, however, has argued more stridently for the primacy of the Anselmian tradition in Scotus. He sets out to challenge the 'standard meaning of willing freely', that is, one rooted in choice between alternatives, by drawing attention to Scotus's claim that God wills in a way at once both necessary and free. Frank has attempted to conclude from this a 'core univocal meaning' for 'willing freely' other than a 'fundamental arbitrariness, a radical freedom of indifference'.[8] So consideration of Scotus on impeccability and freedom in heaven will inevitably lead us to touch on the debate as to what exactly Scotus took freedom to be. So before I turn to the major text in which Scotus treats heavenly impeccability, I shall first consider some of the texts which are of great importance for

---

[5]   D. Langston, *God's Willing Knowledge: The Influence of Scotus' Analysis of Omniscience* (University Park and London: Pennsylvania State University Press, 1986).

[6]   E.g. in W. A. Frank, 'Duns Scotus' Concept of Willing Freely: What Divine Freedom Beyond Choice Teaches Us', *Franciscan Studies* 42 (1982), pp. 68–89.

[7]   J. M. Incandela, 'Duns Scotus and the Experience of Human Freedom', *The Thomist* 56 (1992), pp. 229–56.

[8]   Frank, 'Duns Scotus' Concept of Willing Freely', p. 68.

discerning Scotus's understanding of freedom, as well as his understanding of happiness or beatitude in general.

The main text, and the one from which Frank argues, is number 16 of Scotus's *Quodlibetal Questions*. This question was written up by Scotus himself, and was based on a quodlibetal question which almost certainly took place at Paris in either Advent 1306 or Lent 1307. At a quodlibetal disputation, anyone present could pose a particular question, which the master would then have to 'determine'. In this case Scotus had to determine whether freedom of will and natural necessity were compatible *as regards the same act and object*: Could one and the same act as regards one and the same object be *both* naturally necessary *and* free?[9] Scotus begins his determination by asking whether there is necessity in any act of the will. Once he has established that there is, he will go on to ask whether there is also freedom in the will, and finally whether *natural* necessity can at times co-exist with freedom. That there is necessity of some sort in an act of the will he establishes with the help of two arguments, one based on the spiration of the Holy Spirit (which I shall ignore), and the other on God's own act of beatific love, that act by which God himself is happy.

Scotus holds that there is 'simple necessity' in the act by which God loves himself. This is said to be obvious from the fact that God is necessarily happy or blessed. Given that he is necessarily blessed, he must see and love the beatific object *necessarily*. So he also *loves himself* necessarily. Scotus starts his proof from the fact that an *infinite* will must be related to the *most perfect object* in the most perfect way possible. Given that God's will is infinite, it must be related to the supremely loveable object in the most perfect way that a will *can* relate to such an object. This means that the divine will must love this object

[9]   The question is found in Scotus's *Opera Omnia* (ed. by L. Wadding OFM et al., Lyons: Durand, 1639), XII, pp. 445–73, with a translation by Felix Alluntis OFM and Allan B. Wolter OFM in John Duns Scotus, *God and Creatures. The Quodlibetal Questions* (Princeton and London: Princeton University Press, 1975), pp. 369–87. On textual issues, see *God and Creatures*, pp. xxxi–xxxiii. Cf. Scotus's *Ordinatio*, bk 1, dist. 1, parts 2, q. 2 (Vatican, II, pp. 59–108), bk 4, dist. 49, qq. 9–10 (A. B. Wolter, *Duns Scotus on the Will and Morality*; Washington, DC: Catholic University of America Press, 1986, pp. 182–96).

necessarily and adequately. If it did not, Scotus thinks, it would not be relating to the supremely loveable object in the most perfect way possible, since a yet more perfect way would still be possible, namely, to love it necessarily. Scotus asserts it to be not contradictory for an infinite will to have an infinite act, and hence have a necessary act elicited necessarily with respect to an infinite object. If an infinite will did not have such an act, it would not be a supremely perfect will after all.[10] We saw Suárez take a similar position in the last chapter.

Scotus is keen to distance himself from accepting any arguments for the infinite will necessarily loving an infinite object which would also imply that a *finite* will must also love an infinite object necessarily. Scotus produces three arguments, which he refuses to use to establish that an infinite will loves an infinite object necessarily. He refuses to use them because he thinks that they would also establish that a *finite* will must love an infinite object necessarily, and the latter he holds to be false. The three arguments are generally thought to have been drawn from the works of St Thomas and Henry of Ghent, another thirteenth-century Parisian theologian and one whom Scotus seems to have generally taken as his most serious opponent. I shall mention only one of the three arguments Scotus cites. Like the others, it is meant to apply to the most perfect object, whether it is seen clearly (as in the beatific vision) or only in a general way (presumably as we on earth conceive 'happiness' or 'beatitude' or our 'perfect good' or our 'ultimate end' in a merely general way, without actually seeing that in which the final end in fact consists). The argument goes like this: the will necessarily wills that which includes all goodness, because it cannot fail to love an object in which there is no evil or lack of goodness. Now since the 'ultimate end' *is* such an object without any evil or lack of goodness, the will *necessarily* wills its final end.[11]

Each of the three arguments is said by Scotus not to hold necessarily *of every will*, and he also says that the arguments are also not necessary in themselves. I shall first say a little of how

[10]   *Quodlibetal Questions*, q. 16, n. 2 (pp. 446–7; ET: nn. 4–7, pp. 370–1).
[11]   *Quodlibetal Questions*, q. 16, n. 3 (p. 446; ET: nn. 8–9, p. 371).

Scotus tries to show how the single argument given above does not apply to every will, that is, how it does not apply to *finite* wills. To this end he argues that, of a loveable object, its apprehension by a created intellect, and the created will itself, any one of these three or even all of them could exist without there also being an act of love. To say that any or all three of these could exist without an act of love is not self-contradictory, Scotus asserts. This means that there could be a case of someone faced with an object in itself loveable, who nevertheless does not love it but instead turns away from it. This would of course imply that there are wills which do not necessarily will their 'ultimate end', in that they can turn away from this end rather than make an act of willing it.[12]

In the course of his argument, Scotus also asserts that if a power acted *necessarily* with regard to its object, it would necessarily continue that act *for as long as it was able*. However, the (finite) will, he says, does *not* in fact necessarily continue its act with respect to its ultimate end apprehended in general *for as long as it is able*. In other words, when we think about our 'ultimate end', our 'happiness' or 'beatitude', our 'perfect good' or however we put it, and will it, we are quite able to stop and turn to something else and will that something else, even if we in fact had every opportunity to carry on thinking about and willing our ultimate end. Scotus's point is that if we loved our ultimate end 'necessarily', we would necessarily carry on willing it as long as we possibly could. Consequently, the fact that we do *not* carry on doing this for as long as we possibly can, but instead turn eventually to something else, shows that we do *not* will our ultimate end necessarily.[13]

It is instructive to note that Scotus speaks here only of the finite will of the 'pilgrim', that is, of one's knowing and willing of one's final end while one is *still in this life*. He prescinds from the heavenly case of beatitude, where the finite will is related to the infinite object clearly seen. So when he says that the will does not necessarily continue its act with regard to its final end, he is speaking of 'at least [the will] of the pilgrim' with regard

---

[12] *Quodlibetal Questions*, q. 16, n. 3 (p. 448; ET: n. 12, p. 372).
[13] *Quodlibetal Questions*, q. 16, n. 4 (p. 448; ET: nn. 14–17, pp. 372–3).

to the end apprehended in general in this life. Again, I say that
he prescinds from the case of the will of the blessed who see
God clearly in heaven. All Scotus needs to do for his present
purposes is to show that the argument he is criticising cannot
be used to establish that there is necessity in an act of will
because it would establish that *all* wills love the infinite object
necessarily. To show that it is false that *all* wills do so, Scotus
only needs to have an example that refutes the idea, and the
earthly will of the pilgrim suffices for that. The case of heavenly
beatitude need not bother him. Consequently, he can proceed
towards the problem of the co-existence of freedom and
necessity, having established that there *is* a necessity in an act
of the divine will with regard to an infinite object, by way of
an argument that establishes no more than that, rather than
by an argument that would prove too much, namely, that a
finite will *also* has such a necessary act.

Scotus does not dismiss the three arguments only on the
grounds that they prove something he takes to be untrue. As I
observed above, he also dismisses them because they are not in
themselves necessary arguments. In his attempt to demonstrate
this, he again prescinds from the case of the blessed. The first
of the three arguments, the one I considered above and shall
continue to consider, took as a premise the proposition that the
will necessarily wills that which includes all goodness. From
there it proceeded to establish that the will necessarily loved
the ultimate end, because the latter contained neither evil nor
lack of goodness. Scotus however counters that it is not true
that the will necessarily wills that which includes all goodness.
For such an act to be necessary, he says, not only must there be
such a perfect object, but the power itself must tend necessarily
to that object. He then says that 'whatever be the case with the
created will of the blessed and the supernatural perfection by
which it tends to that perfect object', the created will tends to it
not necessarily but only contingently. The reason is that the
apprehension of the object in a general way cannot be grounds
for necessary love, but Scotus again does not say what he thinks
takes place in the beatific vision.[14] So far this is unsurprising,

---

[14] *Quodlibetal Questions*, q. 16, n. 5 (p. 450; ET: n. 19, p. 374).

but Scotus now qualifies his claim that the will of the pilgrim does not will its final end necessarily.

Scotus is prepared to concede that the will cannot recoil from or refuse such an object that lacks all evil and defect of goodness. Even if it does not will this object necessarily, yet it cannot recoil from or refuse it. The reason is that the will can only will what is loveable and only unwill or nill what is undesirable. The end in question has of course no aspect of undesirability whatsoever. To nill one's end is thus impossible and meaningless. So just as there is something repugnant about willing misery or wretchedness, so there is also something contradictory about nilling one's happiness or beatitude. Scotus says that the latter is perhaps even more repugnant than the former, because while one can perhaps find some grounds for desiring misery, beatitude lacks undesirability in every respect: one simply cannot nill beatitude at all. However, Scotus maintains that the fact that the will cannot recoil from or refuse happiness does not entail that it must necessarily will it. If the will cannot nill beatitude, it does not follow that it can only will it. There is in fact, according to Scotus, the further possibility that the will simply neither wills nor nills this most perfect of objects.[15]

To clarify some of these issues, I want to introduce the distinction encountered in the last chapter between necessity in willing something with regard to the act's specification and with regard to its exercise. Suárez, it will be recalled, said that the blessed necessarily loved their own (created) beatitude with regard to the specification of the act but not with regard to its exercise. In other words the blessed cannot will something contrary to love of their beatitude, but they are able not to exercise the act in question, that is, they do not have to be actually loving their beatitude. Now Scotus has said that one cannot nill one's beatitude, but at the same time one does not necessarily have to will it. Translating this opinion into terms of necessity *quoad specificationem* and necessity *quoad exercitium*, one might say that Scotus teaches that happiness is necessarily willed with regard to specification (one cannot nill it), but is not necessarily willed with regard to exercise (one need not will it).

---

[15] *Quodlibetal Questions*, q. 16, n. 5 (pp. 450–1; ET: nn. 20–1, pp. 374–5).

Moreover, this appears to be not too distant from what St Thomas has to say on the matter, though Scotus is often thought to be opposing Aquinas here. Thomas says that while one necessarily wills happiness *quoad specificationem*, one does not necessarily will it *quoad exercitium*.[16] So, on Thomas's account, while one cannot will against one's beatitude, one does not have to think about beatitude, because the will can turn the mind to something else. The similarity to Scotus is clear. Of course Scotus does want to say that one does *not* necessarily will one's beatitude, and Aquinas that one *does* necessarily will one's beatitude. Their positions are however not so opposed as they seem, since when Scotus *denies* that one necessarily wills one's beatitude, he means that one does not necessarily will it *quoad exercitium*, and when Aquinas *affirms* that one necessarily wills one's beatitude, he means that one wills it only *quoad specificationem*. In other words, both would in fact agree that one necessarily wills one's beatitude with regard to the specification of the act but not with regard to its exercise.

Nevertheless, all disagreement is perhaps not resolved. Recall that Suárez held that in the case of the beatific vision, the blessed loved God necessarily in terms of exercise as well as specification, consciously rejecting Aquinas on this point. Recall also that other commentators, while agreeing with Suárez that God is necessarily loved by the blessed in both ways, interpreted Aquinas as *agreeing* that God was necessarily loved in heaven *quoad exercitium* as well as *quoad specificationem*. When Aquinas said that the will was never necessitated *quoad exercitium*, they took him to be speaking only of this life and not of the next, making the beatific vision an exception to the rule. Suárez, however, took Thomas to be speaking of both heaven and earth. I shall return to Aquinas, but for now simply wish to note once more that Scotus has prescinded from the question of the blessed, but has at least perhaps hinted that not even the blessed are necessitated to love God *quoad exercitium*.

To return then to Scotus's sixteenth quodlibetal question. He has first set out to show that there is some act of the will which

---

[16] *Summa Theologiae*, 1a.2ae., q. 10, a. 2 (Blackfriars edn, vol. XVII, pp. 86–91). Cf. *De Malo*, q. 6, a. un. (Leonine, vol. XXIII, pp. 145–53; ET: R. McInerny in Thomas Aquinas, *Selected Writings*; London: Penguin, 1998, pp. 551–64).

is necessary. He concludes that, whatever be the case with the blessed, whether or not they are necessitated to will their final end by something supernatural, it is 'at least probable' that not every created will is necessitated of its nature to will the end. He holds that this is the case both of the will considered on its own without knowledge, and also of the will considered with regard to its general apprehension of that object in this present life. It is at least certain, however, that the divine will is simply necessitated to love its own goodness, but not creatures, which God wills contingently.[17] Having established this point, Scotus has yet to show that both freedom and necessity in willing can co-exist in the will, before finally addressing the (third) question whether *natural* necessity can ever thus co-exist with freedom.

It is to support his claim that freedom and necessity can co-exist in willing that Scotus brings forward the authority of Augustine and Anselm.[18] The first is a text from Augustine's *Enchiridion*,[19] stating that in the afterlife one will not be able to will evil and yet will not be deprived of free will, but will be freer in that the will is no longer subject to sin. In that state we shall be so happy that not only do we not want to be wretched, but we are quite unable to want to be so: *beati esse sic volumus ut esse miseri non solum nolimus sed nequaquam prorsus velle possimus.* We shall always be unwilling to be wicked, just as in the present life we are unwilling to be unhappy. The second text is of course from Anselm's *De Libertate Arbitrii*,[20] and it says that one who possesses what is appropriate and advantageous in such a way that it *cannot* be lost, is freer than the one who has it in such a way that it *can* be lost. Anselm concludes that the will that cannot cease to be upright is freer than the one which can. In other words, Augustine and Anselm both support the view that freedom can co-exist with necessity. According to Augustine, at the same time that it is necessary that one not will evil, one is not deprived of one's freedom but is freer. According to Anselm, when it is necessary that one not lose righteousness, one is freer. Scotus does not spend any time on explaining what precisely is

---

[17] *Quodlibetal Questions*, q. 16, n. 7 (p. 451; ET: nn. 25–9, pp. 376–7).
[18] *Quodlibetal Questions*, q. 16, n. 8 (pp. 453–4; ET: n. 30, pp. 377–8).
[19] *Enchiridion*, ch. 28, n. 105 (p. 106; ET: pp. 458–9).
[20] *De Libertate Arbitrii*, ch. 1 (I, 208; ET: p. 176).

meant by these authorities. While Suárez was later to dismiss what they say of freedom as equivocation, Scotus simply lets them stand. It is his use in particular of Anselm that has prompted some scholars to suppose that Scotus has a view of freedom ultimately different from indeterminism of the will or 'indifference', or at least that two views of freedom are found in tension in Scotus's thought.

To clarify what he makes of Anselm's view (namely, that not to be able to lose one's righteousness is a greater freedom), I am going to turn to another text, the *Ordinatio*, that is, Scotus's edited version of his lectures on Peter Lombard's *Sentences* given at Oxford between October 1298 and June 1299. In the second book, Scotus considers whether the power to sin comes from God or not.[21] He refers to the fact that Peter Lombard has authorities to cite in favour of the power of sinning coming from God. The authority Scotus himself cites in favour of the power of sinning *not* coming from God is Anselm: to be able to sin is not freedom or any part of freedom.[22] The conclusion drawn from Anselm's statement is that, insofar as free will is from God, free will is *not* the power to sin. But since the ability to sin is not from God for any reason other than that free will comes from him, the implication is that God is in no way the source of the ability to sin.

Scotus's own solution is nuanced. He distinguishes first between the immediate order of potentiality to the act of sinning, and the more remote foundation of this potentiality, by which he means the will itself. God is the source of the latter, which can then act and also be deficient in acting. When one turns to the immediate order of potentiality to the act of sinning, one can distinguish between the (positive) act which is the substratum of a sin, and the lack or defectiveness in the act which makes it a sin. God is the source of the positive act, the sin's substratum, but is in no way the source of the defect, the sinfulness, since in itself the latter is nothing. But though he is not the source of this defect, in these other (nuanced) ways God is indeed the source of the ability to sin. However, Scotus

---

[21]   *Ordinatio*, bk 2, q. 44 (Wolter, *Duns Scotus on the Will and Morality*, pp. 458–9).
[22]   *De Libertate Arbitrii*, ch. 1 (I, 209; ET: p. 176).

is left with the task then of explaining the implication he had drawn from Anselm that the power to sin is in no way from God.[23]

It is here that we have some clue as to how Scotus assimilated Anselm's view of freedom into his own. He replies to Anselm that freedom is a 'pure perfection', and it is on this basis, he asserts, that Anselm assumes it to be in God. However, freedom in human beings is *limited*, and so can be considered in two ways. It can either be considered formally, abstracting from the limitation, in which case it is considered as a pure perfection, or it can be considered as *limited*, that is, as it in fact exists in human beings. So Scotus says that the human will indeed includes the pure perfection of freedom, but also includes it *as limited or finite* and this limitation is not pure perfection. The ability to sin does not pertain to the pure perfection of freedom itself, but only to it *existing as finite*, that is, to the limitation of the perfection. Anselm is explained as saying that the capacity to sin does not pertain to freedom *as a pure perfection*. Anselm's argument that freedom does not include the capacity to sin because *God* is both free and without the capacity to sin, is said to prove no more than that freedom *as a pure perfection* does not include the capacity to sin. As finite, however, freedom includes the capacity to sin. [24]

So Scotus does not straightforwardly adopt Anselm's definition of freedom, though he does assimilate Anselm's view to some degree. Anselm understands freedom to mean the capacity to preserve righteousness, and the highest freedom to mean the inability to lose righteousness, and so the capacity to sin is no part of freedom. The higher freedom he attributes not only to God, but sees as also shared with the blessed. The higher freedom of the blessed means that they are unable to sin. Scotus agrees with Anselm in regard to God, where the pure perfection of freedom exists without limitation, but is unwilling to attribute this higher freedom to finite creatures, even the blessed, it would seem. So the pure perfection of freedom, which includes the inability to sin, is reserved by Scotus to *infinite* being, while it

[23] *Ordinatio*, bk 2, q. 44, n. 1 (pp. 458–61).
[24] *Ordinatio*, bk 2, q. 44, n. 1 (pp. 460–3).

would appear to be characteristic of finite being that it *not* share God's infinite inability to sin, even by grace. Whatever inability to sin the blessed have, it must be something quite other. From all this then, it can be seen that it would be unwise to conclude that Scotus straightforwardly accepted Anselm's views on freedom as his own.

As I said earlier in the chapter, Scotus's use of Anselm has given rise to some scholarly debate as to how Scotus himself *defines* freedom, whether in terms of indeterminacy or as based on Anselm's (higher) freedom in some way. Now given that Scotus is not prepared to share with any creature the perfection of freedom that Anselm is prepared to share with the blessed, it would seem that what Scotus reserves to God's infinite freedom he does not allow to fall within a definition of freedom common to both infinite and finite being. And indeed, for Scotus (as for Anselm), definition of a term takes in only what is *common* to all those beings to which the term is properly applied. When a term is used analogically of God and creatures (such as wisdom), Scotus seeks the definition of the term in a common core of meaning applied to both God and creatures univocally, that is, applied in exactly the same sense. If one stripped away all creaturely imperfections from the application of a term such as wisdom to creatures, one will come to a concept of wisdom, Scotus thinks, that applies to all that is wise, God as well as creatures. When the common concept is then applied specifically to God, it is applied in an infinite or unlimited mode, and if it is applied to a creature, it is applied in a finite or limited mode.

Turning back to *Anselm* on freedom, it is clear that possession of righteousness so as not to be able to lose it is indeed common to the higher freedom of God and the blessed, if not to the lower freedom of the fallen (who only share in common the ability to preserve it, even though in their case it is not there to be preserved). But, as we have seen, *Scotus* seems to reserve this inability only to God's freedom, that is, freedom in an infinite mode. Given that fact, it must be concluded that Anselm's views on freedom are not simply adopted by Scotus as his own. Rather Scotus applies Anselm's definition of the higher freedom only to freedom as it exists in the infinite being of God, and not to the finite freedom as it exists in human creatures, even when blessed by the beatific vision. So Scotus does not straight-forwardly adopt Anselm's views, and does not even appear to adopt Anselm's general definition as his own univocal core meaning of freedom.[25]

Returning once again to the *Quodlibetal Questions*, Scotus has used the authority of Augustine and the authority of Anselm to argue that there can be freedom and necessity in the same act. However, in the third and final article of the question, he will eventually deny that freedom and *natural* necessity can co-exist in the same act with respect to the same object. The will acts where it acts necessarily not with *natural* necessity but with another kind of necessity. Of the different kinds of necessity he recognises, among those applied to God by Scotus are the following: natural necessity, by which God necessarily lives; the necessity by which he necessarily knows, which stems from the intellectual object determining the intellect to know it; the necessity by which he necessarily spirates the Holy Spirit, a kind of natural necessity which does not precede the will's act but accompanies it; and finally the necessity by which he necessarily loves himself, a necessity distinct from natural necessity.[26]

It is for the last of these necessities that Scotus presents his own arguments. Scotus argues that while it has already been established that God necessarily wills his own goodness, it is also the case that he is *free* in willing his own goodness, and consequently there is an act, namely God's willing of his own goodness, in which freedom and necessity co-exist. Given that he has already established the *necessity* of this act, it is its *freedom* that he now needs to argue for. In this he differs from Suárez who, as we have seen, denies that this act of the will is free but terms it necessary only. Scotus argues for the act's freedom first from the fact that the divine will contingently wills those things which it orders to the divine goodness. This contingent willing must be free in order to be contingent. The will therefore, being

[25] For a critique of Frank's particular arguments in detail, see D. Langston, 'Did Scotus Embrace Anselm's Notion of Freedom?', *Medieval Philosophy and Theology* 5 (1996), pp. 145–59.

[26] *Quodlibetal Questions*, q. 16, nn. 11–18 (pp. 455–9; ET: nn. 35–50, pp. 380–7).

the *same basic power*, must also be free when it necessarily wills its own goodness. In other words, the will freely wills both its own goodness necessarily *and* what it orders to itself contingently.[27]

Furthermore, God's willing his own goodness is an action to do with the ultimate end, and therefore with the most perfect of actions. Since freedom pertains to the perfection of such an action, this necessary willing must also be free.[28] Moreover, freedom is an intrinsic condition of the will. Since an intrinsic condition of a power cannot be opposed to perfection in acting (in this case, the necessity of God's willing his own goodness), freedom cannot be opposed to that necessity. Scotus is not particularly clear on how this necessity can co-exist with freedom, and indeed refuses to seek a reason for something for which no reason, he says, can be given. However he is convinced that the two *must* co-exist, because this act must be necessary *and* it must be free.[29] Where this leaves the precise Scotistic definition of freedom, the core of meaning of 'freedom' common to both God and creatures, is again not particularly clear. One addition at the end of the article on the co-existence of necessity and freedom suggests that 'choice' remains the core meaning, since it speaks of God as it were 'electably eliciting' this act and persevering in it as something chosen – *eligibiliter elicit*.[30] But for the moment at least, that scholarly debate remains unresolved. In this chapter, however, we have established something concerning God's infinite freedom and something concerning finite human freedom, at least as it is exercised in this world. To the freedom of the blessed, in Scotus's thought, we turn in the next chapter.

[27] *Quodlibetal Questions*, q. 16, n. 8 (p. 454; ET: n. 31, p. 378).

[28] I have followed here the reading of the text given by Wadding, and Alluntis and Wolter. However, Frank, 'Duns Scotus' Concept of Willing Freely', has argued from three of the earliest manuscripts that *libertas* (freedom) should read *firmitas* (steadfastness), and has argued from this for a Scotistic univocal definition of freedom along Anselmian lines as *firmitas*. Although Langston rejects Frank's conclusions, he does not reject the *firmitas* reading of the text.

[29] *Quodlibetal Questions*, q. 16, nn. 8–9 (p. 454; ET: nn. 32–3, pp. 378–9).

[30] *Quodlibetal Questions*, q. 16, n. 10 (p. 455; ET: n. 34, p. 380). See Langston, 'Did Scotus Embrace Anselm's Notion of Freedom?', p. 156.

4

Beatitude, Perpetuity
and Impeccability:
Duns Scotus

While Suárez was to give separate consideration to both
perpetuity and impeccability, when commenting on St Thomas's
Summa, Scotus had given separate consideration only to perpetuity, when commenting on Peter Lombard's *Sentences*.[1]
Impeccability is raised by Scotus only in the context of his
attempt to show that the *perpetuity* of beatitude has no intrinsic
cause but is caused only by the extrinsic providence of God.
Scotus's dominant concern seems to be to preserve God's infinite
freedom as the source of beatitude's perpetuity against any finite
competitor. We saw in the previous chapter how Scotus did
not wish the necessity he thought proper to infinite freedom to
be conceded to finite freedom. Similarly we now find him eager
to maintain what he takes to be infinite freedom's special pre-
rogatives in the face of the pretensions of any pretended finite
cause of heaven's perpetuity.

Scotus's main question is whether 'security' pertains to
beatitude, which amounts to asking whether beatitude is
perpetual. Scotus has no doubt that beatitude *is* perpetual, and
has no difficulty in demonstrating this from various authorities,
scriptural and otherwise. Next he lists what are nevertheless
points of doubt, and the first of these is the identity of the *cause*
of perpetuity.[2] He goes on to present and reject three theories
of the causation of perpetuity. The first takes beatitude to be
formally perpetual, the second argues that beatitude is perpetual

[1]   *Ordinatio*, bk 4, dist. 49, q. 6 (Wadding, vol. X, pp. 428–78).
[2]   *Ordinatio*, bk 4, dist. 49, q. 6, nn. 1–3 (X, pp. 428–9).

51

on account of the perfection of its *object* (that object being of course God), and the third that perpetuity arises from the necessity of the acts of the blessed brought about by the *habits* of the 'light of glory' and charity inhering in the intellect and will respectively.[3]

In his response to the first theory, Scotus rejects anything finite as a candidate for the cause of perpetuity, and this is done explicitly in the name of preserving the role of God's infinite freedom. The first theory argues that beatitude is formally perpetual, maintaining that beatitude is necessary *of itself*, and so therefore cannot but be perpetual. Perpetuity is thus an essential property of beatitude (although it of course has its ultimate source in an extrinsic cause, that is, God).[4] The three arguments in favour of this theory will be rejected by Scotus, because they are seen by him as derogating from God's infinite freedom. Again, the argument Scotus puts against the theory speaks firmly in favour of this divine freedom. This argument starts from the fact that 'created beatitude' is an 'accident' inhering in a subject. In other words, beatitude is a property of the blessed soul or beatified nature. As such a property, the argument goes, it can be no less *dependent* than the subject of which it is a property. Now the subject in question is of course dependent on God's contingent conservation of it in being. In other words, the subject only exists because God freely chooses to make it exist. Given that this subject, namely, the beatified soul, has no strictly necessary being, even less can the accident inhering in it, namely, beatitude, have such necessary being.

Scotus considers the view that once beatitude has been produced, it might be said to remain necessarily in a sense, if not absolutely necessarily, given that the nature it beatifies remains in being. However, against this it is urged that God could instead conserve the soul in being, while having ceased to conserve its beatitude, because God had previously conserved the soul in being without its having possessed this particular property. The relationship of the property of beatitude to God just cannot have a greater necessity than the relationship of the

---

[3]   *Ordinatio*, bk 4, dist. 49, q. 6, n. 4 (X, p. 430).
[4]   *Ordinatio*, bk 4, dist. 49, q. 6, n. 5 (X, p. 430).

property's subject to God. Just as God had once conserved this nature in being without it being blessed, so, once it has become blessed, he can again conserve the nature itself in being while allowing its blessedness to come to naught. Such is the dependence of beatitude and therefore of its perpetuity on God's conserving power.

Scotus is, however, prepared to concede that some things, including beatitude, have 'incorruptible' being, without their being absolutely necessary. Scotus says that God alone is formally necessary, with everything else contingent. Of these contingent beings, however, those are said to be incorruptible which cannot be destroyed by any other creature. Such incorruptible creatures can be annihilated only if God should choose not to conserve them in being. This is the sense in which Scotus concedes incorruptibility to beatitude. Beatitude can be taken out of existence *only* by the Creator himself. As incorruptible in this sense, the perpetuity of beatitude is derived not from finite beatitude itself, but from God who conserves it in being.[5]

From this position, Scotus can reject those arguments which he adduces in favour of the first theory. For example, the first argument is that beatitude, as the supreme perfection of a spiritual nature, will be formally incorruptible and therefore perpetual. Beatitude is envisaged as a perfection proper to an incorruptible nature, just as luminosity was a proper perfection of the stars, which the medievals held to be incorruptible bodies. So just as the heavenly bodies of themselves always have their own proper perfection of luminosity, so beatitude has its own proper perpetuity.[6] Scotus, however, has distinguished necessary being from incorruptible being. The incorruptibility of beatitude simply means that only God but no creature can annihilate it, so that incorruptibility itself cannot account for beatitude's perpetuity. The causation of the latter remains the privilege of God's conserving power.[7]

So much for the first theory's first argument. The second argument appeals to the idea that something incorruptible is

5   *Ordinatio*, bk 4, dist. 49, q. 6, n. 6 (X, p. 431).
6   *Ordinatio*, bk 4, dist. 49, q. 6, n. 5 (X, p. 430).
7   *Ordinatio*, bk 4, dist. 49, q. 6, n. 7 (X, p. 431).

formed when its material or matter is formed by a form which removes from it *every privation*. The second argument supposes that the matter from which the heavenly bodies were made was so completely actualised by the forms in question that the heavenly bodies themselves had no further potential for receiving other forms. Their potential for such change had been so completely realised that the heavens were incorruptible. What is suggested by the second argument is that beatitude likewise removes every privation from the nature it perfects, and an incorruptible unity of the blessed with their beatitude will result. Beatitude, as the ultimate actuality in its own order, will remove all imperfection and potentiality to a degree greater than in the case of the heavens and their form.

This reasoning is intended to be confirmed from a comparison of the ultimate intrinsic end of human beings (their beatitude) to their extrinsic end (God). This extrinsic end, since it includes in itself the perfection of every other end 'in a higher way' (*eminenter*), removes from itself every privation or lack. Similarly, an ultimate intrinsic end, such as (created) beatitude, would have a comparable perfection, and likewise remove from itself every privation. It would hence constitute with the subject it perfects a composite of beatitude itself and the beatified subject, which would be formally and intrinsically incorruptible, and the blessed subject would also be united to its extrinsic end. If union were here not perpetual, a privation would remain. This privation, the potential to lose beatitude, has however been removed by the perfection of that perfect intrinsic end.[8]

Scotus, however, does not accept the view that even the form of the heavens removes from them every privation. On Scotus's view, there is no (finite) form that can remove from its matter every possibility of receiving a new form. Only a form which somehow already contains that 'new' form 'in a higher way' is without any such privation. If the first form does not contain these further forms in a higher way, then its matter will remain able to receive them in the future. And if it can receive them in the future, every privation will *not* have been removed, because it can still undergo change by receiving new forms. Scotus holds

8   *Ordinatio*, bk 4, dist. 49, q. 6, n. 5 (X, p. 430).

that the form of the heavens does not include all forms in itself *in any way*, not even in a 'higher way', and so the heavens simply do not have every lack or privation removed from them, on account of the fact that their matter is open to receive new forms. The intellect is another example of a finite form that does *not* remove every privation from its matter such that matter and form constitute an incorruptible unity. If this is not the case with the intellect, which is a higher form than the form of the heavens, then neither will it be the case with the form of the heavens, which is a lower form than the intellect.[9]

Again we see the distinction between the infinite and the finite asserting itself once more. Only God, the infinite form, is without every imperfection, and only this infinite form contains in itself all other forms 'in a higher way'. The attempted confirmation of the reasoning of the second argument is thus also rejected by Scotus. Scotus responds that an intrinsic (and therefore finite) end never formally removes *every* privation. Only the extrinsic end lacks every defect in itself, on account of its being formally *infinite*. An intrinsic end is only finite, and as such does not contain the perfection that the extrinsic end does. Scotus considers the possibility that the intrinsic end will still remove all imperfection because it unites its subject to the *extrinsic* end, which itself is responsible for removing all privation. Scotus concedes only that, just as white, while present, removes blackness, so the intrinsic end will remove imperfection *while it remains present*. The intrinsic end is not, however, necessary in itself: that belongs to the extrinsic end.[10] Hence the intrinsic end of beatitude can still be brought out of existence, though only by God. Its perpetuity is caused by God and is not derived from the intrinsic end of beatitude itself.

The third argument is based on the incorruptibility of that nature itself to which beatitude is given. If beatitude is only 'possible', that is, if it could be removed, then the blessed, having lost their blessedness, would themselves remain in existence on account of their natural incorruptibility, but would have become 'miserable' or 'wretched'. Knowing this always to be a

⁹ *Ordinatio*, bk 4, dist. 49, q. 6, n. 7 (X, p. 431).
¹⁰ *Ordinatio*, bk 4, dist. 49, q. 6, n. 8 (X, p. 432).

possibility, the blessed could in fact never be truly blessed, because they would always lack something that they would want, namely that they should never become miserable. In saying that the blessed would not have 'whatever they want' (*quicquid vult*), the argument alludes to Augustine's saying that the blessed have all that they want. The point here is that the blessed would not have something which they would want, and so would not be blessed. Given that they are blessed, they must have whatever they want, including that they never become miserable, thereby making perpetuity essential to beatitude.[11]

Scotus's reply hinges on the beatified nature remaining the same nature. Given that it does remain the same in nature, it will always remain capable of both beatitude and misery. It would therefore be possible for this nature, on ceasing to be beatified, to become miserable. To the objection that the nature would therefore not have whatever it wanted and thus not be blessed at all, Scotus replies with his standard interpretation of Augustine's saying. Scotus takes this saying to imply that the blessed have all they will, not 'distributively' but rather 'unitively'. In other words, they possess whatever they want not as many beatific acts of will with varied objects, but possess it by a single beatific act of will with God as its object. As this object, God contains 'in a higher way everything that is rightly willable' (*eminenter habuit omne recte volibile*).[12] Presumably, what is rightly willable will include at least the *fact* of beatitude's perpetuity. What is at issue for Scotus is the *cause* of this perpetuity. Scotus presumably thinks that, as long as perpetuity is assured, it need not be necessary to perpetual beatitude that its perpetuity be part of the formal notion of beatitude, perpetuity being derived from God's extrinsic providence alone. What is of interest to us here, however, is that an intrinsic cause for perpetuity has been rejected not just on the ground of defending the prerogative of divine freedom, but also on the ground of the beatified nature remaining what it was before.

---

[11]   *Ordinatio*, bk 4, dist. 49, q. 6, n. 5 (X, p. 430). See Augustine, *De Trinitate*, bk 13, ch. 5(8) (50A, p. 393; ET: E. Hill OP, *The Trinity*; Brooklyn, NY: New City Press, 1991, p. 349).

[12]   *Ordinatio*, bk 4, dist. 49, q. 6, n. 8 (X, p. 432).

The nature of the blessed remains capable of not having beatitude, just as it always was before beatitude was conferred. Presumably a role for the freedom of the human will is implied here that rules out an intrinsic cause of perpetuity, but we shall return to this matter in due course, and there ends our account of Scotus's rejection of the first theory and its three arguments.

Of the three theories, the second is most immediately relevant to our purposes, since it bears most resemblance to the theories of Suárez, which we considered in Chapter 2. The second theory is that the perpetuity of beatitude arises from the fact that the will necessarily enjoys the beatific object clearly seen, in which there is no evil or lack of good. Given that the will must necessarily enjoy such an object clearly seen in this way, its happiness must go on perpetually.[13] Scotus notes that he has already made a reply to this position in book 1 of his commentary on Lombard. There he puts forward substantially the same position as appears later in book 4 of the commentary and also in the quodlibetal question I analysed in the last chapter.[14] For Scotus it is simply part of what the will is that it can both will and not will. Even if the will cannot nill its own beatitude, it does not follow that it must necessarily will it: the will can always simply not will. Although in the *Quodlibetal Questions*, Scotus often prescinded from considering the case of the beatific vision where the beatific object is clearly seen, in his commentary on Peter Lombard he has his arguments count for the next life too. He includes both a hypothetical situation in which a soul had the vision of God but not love of him (beatitude consisting for Scotus formally in the latter), and the truly beatific situation in which there are both acts present. In no case does Scotus allow that the perfection of the object clearly seen will necessitate an act of the will: the will always retains its power for not willing its object.

Returning to the issue of perpetuity, Scotus says that even if the intellect were naturally necessitated by its object, the will

---

[13] *Ordinatio*, bk 4, dist. 49, q. 6, n. 4 (X, p. 430).
[14] The texts from the commentary are *Ordinatio*, bk 1, dist. 1, part 2, q. 2 (Vatican, II, pp. 59–108), bk 4, dist. 49, qq. 9–10 (Wolter, *Duns Scotus on the Will and Morality*, pp. 182–96).

would still not be. However, the necessity of seeing God in the beatific vision is in fact *not* a simple necessity. It is necessary that the blessed behold God *only on the condition that* the object itself, that is, God, moves it, and God moves it only *voluntarily and contingently*. Hence there is no simple necessity involved in the act of vision. The infinite freedom of God is once more at issue: vision cannot be necessary precisely because it is *freely* that God moves the intellect. But the freedom of the finite will is also at issue, as well as the divine will. The will is said to enjoy its object *contingently*, and is itself responsible for bringing the memory to bear on the beatific object. Both infinite and finite freedom come together for the same conclusion: the will is not necessitated by the perfection of the object clearly seen. The will always remains free not to will, even in heaven. Perpetuity cannot therefore arise from any necessitation of acts on the part of their object.[15]

The third theory takes the intellect to be necessitated to see God on account of the heavenly 'light of glory', and the will to be necessitated to love God on account of the consummate charity proper to heaven. The light of glory and charity are said to elevate the blessed not only to see and to love God, but to see and to love him *necessarily*. Given this necessity, beatitude will continue perpetually.[16] Scotus, however, does not think these two habits capable of bringing about such necessity and consequently not capable of being the cause of perpetuity. Such a theory, Scotus thinks, would give to these habits a certain priority over the powers they modify, a priority which in fact must belong to the powers themselves. While the powers of intellect and will are in fact primary and their habits secondary, this theory would have the habits render the powers of intellect and will necessary, making the habits the primary causes in the causation of the acts of knowledge and love. But given that it is powers that make use of habits to act and not the other way around, the theory must be rejected. The primary cause of something is never determined to act by anything secondary, and so cannot be necessitated by anything secondary. So those

15   *Ordinatio*, bk 4, dist. 49, q. 6, n. 9 (X, p. 433).
16   *Ordinatio*, bk 4, dist. 49, q. 6, n. 4 (X. p. 430).

habits of which the powers make use cannot necessitate those powers to act. Consequently, the habits cannot necessitate the beatific acts and so cannot in turn cause beatitude's perpetuity.

Scotus also presents two further arguments why the light of glory and charity cannot be the cause of perpetuity. One is based on Scotus's Mariology. The Blessed Virgin is said to have had a greater charity while on earth than any of the blessed have in heaven. Now given that her charity on earth, though so great, did not necessitate the beatific enjoyment of God, even while she was engaged in contemplation, then neither can the habit of charity in heaven necessitate such a beatific act. The other argument is based on the fact that the intellect is commanded by the will. It is therefore the will which either does or does not command the act of vision. However, the will would not be able to be such a cause of the act of vision, if the vision had been necessitated by the light of glory. So the fact that it is the will's role to command the intellect's act of vision excludes the possibility of the light of glory necessitating the beatific vision or beatitude's perpetuity. In conclusion, Scotus denies that any strict necessity arises from any habits, and the only necessity he will concede is in a limited sense in regard to the light of glory, which *inclines* the intellect to the act of vision.[17] Two finite pretenders, the light of glory and consummate charity, are thus excluded from being the cause of perpetuity, and the infinite freedom of God is left once more in full command.

Before going on to how Scotus introduces the notion of impeccability into the question, we should recall that Scotus might have asked whether perpetuity could have been caused through an act of will on the part of the blessed that was at once both necessary *and* free. In the last chapter we saw how Scotus was prepared to say that there was an act of the will in which both necessity and freedom coincided. If such was the case, could not the beatific love of the blessed be such an act, with perpetuity arising from the necessity of that act, a necessity itself dependent on the infinite perfection of the object clearly

[17] *Ordinatio*, bk 4, dist. 49, q. 6, n. 9 (X, p. 433).

seen? Scotus's answer would lie of course in the fact that he concedes such an act only to the infinite will of God. No finite act of will can combine freedom and necessity in this way. So only God's beatitude could be perpetual by way of the perfection of its object. This sheds further light on how the distinction between finite and infinite being is crucial to so much of Scotus's thinking.

It is both the infinite freedom of God and the finite freedom of the human will that Scotus has been at pains to preserve in the question of perpetuity. Nothing finite could be responsible for the causation of perpetuity, only the infinite freedom of God: the finite cannot trespass on the preserve of the infinite. Again the freedom of the blessed must be preserved, but in excluding the possibility of a beatific act at once both free and necessary, it is very much *finite* freedom, human finitude, that is being preserved. The heights of divine freedom cannot be shared with human freedom, even in beatitude: the finite once more cannot trespass on the preserve of the infinite. We saw in Chapter 2 how Suárez was hesitant to allow a single act which was necessary in regard to its primary object but free in regard to its secondary objects to be shared by the infinite will with finite wills: only God can will one thing necessarily and other things freely by the same act. Here we see something similar in Scotus: only God can will the *same* object both necessarily and freely, and such can never be allowed of a finite creature.

Scotus concludes then that it is 'the divine will alone' which confers perpetuity on the perfection of the nature it likewise freely causes to be. Having established that the cause of perpetuity is nothing intrinsic to the blessed, Scotus then raises a 'doubt'. This *dubium* is how 'blessed Michael' can be impeccable, given the absence of any intrinsic cause of beatitude's perpetuity. Given the non-existence of such a cause, the blessed would be able not to enjoy God (that is, to cease from enjoying him) and thus to sin: *per consequens potest non frui, et ita peccare*. Scotus thus seems to be in no doubt that to cease from enjoying God is sinful, probably regarding it as a sin of omission, given that the command to love God with one's whole being is still effective in heaven, indeed is fulfilled in all of its conditions only there.[18] The *dubium*, however, is that this would rule out impeccability, and impeccability is supported by the authority of Augustine. Scotus quotes Augustine's *Contra Maximinum* to the effect that the blessed are unable to sin though not by nature but by the grace of God[19] and the *Enchiridion* to the effect that the soul, just as it nills unhappiness in this life, nills iniquity in the next, and that not only do we not will to be wretched but we are never able to will wretchedness.[20] The doubt concerning Scotus's whole line on the cause of perpetuity is that it will leave the blessed able to will sin such that they are not impeccable.

Scotus's task then is to develop a theory of impeccability that is at once consonant with his 'extrinsic' theory of perpetuity but which also satisfies his authorities on impeccability. I shall first set out how he attempts to achieve this, and then ask how his account would appear to those who would be unprepared to weaken impeccability in any way, and to others, such as Donnelly, who are concerned to uphold human freedom in heaven. Scotus begins his reply to the doubt by analysing the proposition that 'the blessed are impeccable' in a number of ways.[21] The first way is to take the proposition in its 'composed' sense. In other words, the proposition is understood to mean that a blessed soul cannot *at the very same moment* be both blessed and sinning. Scotus indeed agrees that one cannot be both at the same time blessed and in the act of sin. So in the 'composed sense' of the proposition, the blessed just are impeccable.

There is also, however, a 'divided sense' of the proposition that the one who remains blessed has no power or possibility of sinning. The question here presumes that a soul could at one moment be blessed and at the next moment sin. At the moment that the soul was blessed, it could not have at that moment

[18] *Ordinatio*, bk 4, dist. 49, q. 6, n. 10 (X, p. 454). Cf. bk 3, suppl. dist. 27, a. 3 (Wolter, *Duns Scotus on the Will and Morality*, pp. 440–1).
[19] *Ordinatio*, bk 4, dist. 49, q. 6, n. 10 (X, p. 454), citing bk 2, ch. 12 (J. P. Migne, *Patrologia Latina*, vol. XLII, col. 768).
[20] *Ordinatio*, bk 4, dist. 49, q. 6, n. 10 (X, p. 455), citing ch. 28, n. 105 (p. 106; ET: pp. 458–9).
[21] *Ordinatio*, bk 4, dist. 49, q. 6, n. 11 (X, p. 455).

been sinning, though it could sin at the next moment. Given this scenario, how are we to understand the proposition that as long as it remained blessed, the soul then had no power to sin? Scotus offers two possible interpretations of this proposition. On the first interpretation there is something *intrinsic* to the blessed which excludes the power of sinning. On the second interpretation there is a cause *extrinsic* to the blessed which excludes the *proximate* power of sinning. The first interpretation Scotus rejects: there is nothing intrinsic in the present life that excludes the power of sinning, and there will be nothing intrinsic in the next. In other words, the will simply remains what it was before, that is, free to sin. Presumably, if Scotus had earlier concluded that there was something intrinsic to the blessed that caused the perpetuity of their beatitude, he would have identified that cause as also an intrinsic cause of their impeccability. However, Scotus has already rejected any intrinsic cause of perpetuity, and now he also rejects any intrinsic cause of impeccability.

The second interpretation of the divided sense had only the *proximate* power of sinning excluded from the blessed. The implication is that while the extrinsic cause at issue (God) excludes the proximate power of sinning from the blessed, it leaves their *remote* power for sinning intact. Scotus presents an analogy to illustrate this point. The power of sight naturally has the capacity to see. Even were some extrinsic cause to rule out its proximate capacity for seeing some object by interposing some perpetual distance between the power and its object, the remote capacity for seeing would nevertheless remain. Scotus's particular example is a perpetual obstacle placed by an extrinsic cause, such that the obstacle prevented the eye of someone in hell from seeing the empyrean heaven (the heaven of light beyond the stars). Such an eye would be unable to see the empyrean heaven with regard to the eye's proximate power (on account of the perpetual obstacle) but would retain its intrinsic remote power for sight because no intrinsic cause had removed it.

In a similar way, 'blessed Michael' would retain his remote power for sinning, but on account of an extrinsic cause (God's prevenient will) his proximate power for sinning would have been removed. So the blessed would be peccable with regard to their remote power but impeccable with regard to their proximate power.[22] In other words, they would be able to sin because they always have free will, but God prevents them from exercising this capacity. In the analogy of the eye, the extrinsic cause perpetually placed distance or an obstacle between the eye and its object. In the case of the blessed, how does God prevent the blessed from exercising their freedom to sin? His grace preserves and conserves the blessed in their beatific act of enjoyment, such that they never exercise their remote power of not enjoying or sinning: the superior cause (God) prevents a change of will. It is here that Scotus's solution may prove especially unattractive to a libertarian like Donnelly, as we shall see. However there is also the question whether this account of impeccability would prove acceptable to impeccability's other proponents.

Scotus evidently believes that, even though he accepts peccability with regard to the remote power for sinning, his account nevertheless satisfies the authorities on impeccability. But, just as he took Anselm as an authority on the nature of freedom and transformed Anselm's doctrine even as he took it over, so he may possibly do the same with Augustine on impeccability. In *Contra Maximinum* Augustine said that the blessed were impeccable not by nature but by divine 'grace'. Augustine believes that while God cannot sin by nature, impeccable human beings are such not by their own nature but only by God's gift. Scotus goes on to interpret what Augustine must mean here by 'grace' with the help of an application of his own distinction between remote and proximate powers.[23] He interprets 'by grace' more precisely as referring in particular to God's extrinsic providence to the exclusion of any intrinsic gift of grace. So on Scotus's interpretation of Augustine, it is by his extrinsic causality that God removes the proximate power for sinning, while leaving intact the natural remote power. Now it is clear from his writings that Augustine held that in heaven the blessed were 'unable to sin'. Scotus interprets this inability

---

[22] *Ordinatio*, bk 4, dist. 49, q. 6, n. 11 (X, p. 455).
[23] *Ordinatio*, bk 4, dist. 49, q. 6, n. 12 (X, p. 455).

with regard to proximate ability but not with regard to remote ability. It is arguable, however, that Augustine would have accepted impeccability with regard to both powers, had the distinction been put to him in this regard. Moreover, as we saw in connection with Suárez, Augustine defends the compatibility of freedom with impeccability by arguing for a *higher freedom* in heaven, not by appealing to the continuation of a remote as opposed to a proximate power.

The other Augustinian authority cited by Scotus was the passage from the *Enchiridion* concerning the nilling of unhappiness in this life and of iniquity in the next, which he also used in the *Quodlibetal Questions*, as we saw in the previous chapter: just as the soul nills unhappiness in this life, so it always nills iniquity in the next. Scotus first says that Augustine does not assert that we *necessarily* nill unhappiness in this life and thus *necessarily* nill iniquity in the future. Neither of these is true, Scotus says, in terms of the elicited act (in other words, there is no necessity of exercise here). What Augustine is saying, according to Scotus, is that just as we now *habitually* nill unhappiness, so in the future we shall *habitually* nill iniquity. To do something habitually does not imply that it is done necessarily, so from this reading Scotus can take a weaker view of impeccability, although (as we have seen in the previous two chapters) a wider reading of Augustine shows that he in fact held a stronger view of impeccability. Scotus wants to preserve peccability in heaven with respect to the remote power, so he has interpreted Augustine to mean that the blessed habitually rather than necessarily nill iniquity. Scotus concedes that in this life we *cannot* will unhappiness (which Augustine also says in the passage in question), though not because we necessarily exercise an act of nilling it, but because unhappiness as such simply cannot be an act of the will. There is of course a sense in which we can will *iniquity*, because we can will it as involved in sin.

Scotus's point of comparison between this life and the next turns out to have to do not with what *cannot* be done but what is *in fact* done. Scotus concludes that just as we now never will unhappiness but only nill it habitually, in the future we shall never will iniquity but always habitually nill it. The point of comparison is not from being *unable* to will unhappiness in this life to being *unable* to will iniquity in the next. For Scotus, Augustine's point of comparison is not what *cannot* be done, but what de facto is not done. Scotus takes Augustine to be saying that just as we do not in fact will unhappiness as such in this life, so we shall not will iniquity in the next – de facto.[24] Whether or not this is a correct interpretation of what Augustine meant (and, as I have said, wider reading suggests it is incorrect) is only one matter. Of course, even if Scotus has transformed Augustine in his interpretation of the authorities, it may be that Scotus's view is simply right and Augustine's wrong. On the other hand, the view of impeccability Scotus propounds may have problems in its own right, and not just as an interpretation of Augustine.

Scotus's weaker view of impeccability hangs on a continuing remote ability to sin on the basis that the will can simply will or not will. Scotus does not allow that one can ever nill one's beatitude, but he does maintain that we need not will, in terms of the exercise of the act. So once one has made a beatific act of will in heaven, one remains free subsequently to refrain from that act in terms of one's remote power. Having loved God in the beatific vision, though the soul cannot make an act of hatred of God, it nevertheless has the remote power to cease to love him. It is difficult, however, to see how such a refraining from an act of love of God would not be equivalent to rejecting him. The beatified soul knows God as perfect in every respect without any lack of good. The beatified soul knows that God is its supreme good. It is also aware of the command to love God with all its being, now truly possible to fulfil on account of the removal of all the effects of sin and the demands of earthly life.[25] How are to we make sense of such a soul turning its intellect and will away from God to something less? Scotus seems to be saying that though one cannot reject God or recoil from him, one can nevertheless cease to place one's happiness in him. But how in this situation can ceasing to will not be

---

[24] *Ordinatio*, bk 4, dist. 49, q. 6, n. 12 (X, p. 455).
[25] Cf. *Ordinatio*, bk 3, suppl. dist. 27, a. 3 (Wolter, *Duns Scotus on the Will and Morality*, pp. 440–1).

equivalent to nilling? Scotus would no doubt concede that for the most part such a soul would not turn away from its happiness. However, he would also assert that the continuation of the free nature of the soul implies that it just must retain the power to cease from willing. But it seems difficult to see how this heavenly ceasing from willing could be anything other than nilling, and the latter Scotus has altogether ruled out.

When we set out to examine Scotus's doctrine, however, it was with the purpose of asking whether he, as a celebrated voluntarist, might offer a theory of heavenly impeccability that also preserved freedom in heaven in such an attractive way that even someone like Donnelly, having been persuaded of the orthodoxy of impeccability, might be won over to it. As we have seen, Scotus has a weaker view of impeccability than others such as Suárez, and this weaker view is bound up with a continuing remote power for sinning, even though the proximate power is excluded. But could Scotus's solution prove attractive to someone already attracted to the modern 'libertarian' conception of freedom which Donnelly had wished to see continued in heaven? That Scotus would almost certainly fail here can be seen from an objection that Scotus himself raises against his own position: If God's extrinsic causality preserves the beatific act in being, how can that determination of the creature's act not but destroy its freedom?

According to the objection, if another cause, whether superior or inferior, determines the will, it removes from it its indifference: the will has been determined one way. To determine the will away from something would thus go against its nature, because the determining cause would have removed its (natural) indifference. For the objector, it is no less contrary to nature for God to determine the will than it would be for a habit to determine it necessarily. God of course is a superior cause of the will, and a *superior* cause would no doubt remove this indifference from the will, thinks the objector, even more so than would an *inferior* cause.[26] The objection is one of determinism. Does Scotus's position not end up removing the very freedom of the blessed he has wished to defend, because

[26]   *Ordinatio*, bk 4, dist. 49, q. 6, n. 13 (Wadding, X, p. 456).

God is determining the continuation of the beatific act and so excluding the possibility of sin? Moreover, does this not render the beatific act itself incapable of praise and not truly voluntary, because the will has had removed from it the power of acting and not acting?[27]

Scotus's defence would perhaps be as alarming to someone like Donnelly as would be the very suspicion of determinism in the first place. The objection's assertion that freedom is removed by a determining *superior* cause as much as by a determining *inferior* cause hints at Scotus's answer. It is Scotus's doctrine that a metaphysically superior cause differs here from a metaphysically inferior cause. Scotus begins his reply by clarifying the nature of the causation proper to a free agent. He is of the opinion that when, in its own order, the will causes some effect, that effect proceeds from its cause *contingently*: the effect itself must be *contingent*. What therefore is repugnant to the will's freedom is that the (inferior) effect produced by it be not contingent. Note however that nothing has been implied here about the role a cause *superior* to the will might possibly take. A cause that is *superior* to the will, one which the will itself has not determined, *can* determine the will to act in a certain way. In his own order of causality, God, undoubtedly a superior cause, can determine the continuation of the will's act of willing God in heaven without removing the will's natural freedom. Thus God's manner of causation in its own superior order is not repugnant to the (free) nature of the will.

Scotus is distinguishing here between how a superior determining cause is related to the agent whose effect it determines, and how an inferior determining cause is related to this agent. This enables him to respond directly to the objection, which ran superior and inferior together. Scotus concedes that it would certainly be contrary to the nature of the free agent for its act to be determined by a metaphysically inferior cause. However, Scotus thinks it would not be contrary to its nature for its act to be determined by a *superior* cause. It seems that Scotus supposes that an inferior cause can determine the act of the superior cause only by affecting that agent's (free)

[27] *Ordinatio*, bk 4, dist. 49, q. 6, n. 13 (X, p. 457).

nature. In contrast, a superior cause need not affect the nature of the will and render it unfree, but determine it to act without undermining its own natural freedom. God would thus determine the will to act precisely through the will's own (free) nature. The objection had supposed that the superior cause would remove freedom *even more* than would an inferior determining cause. Instead, it seems that Scotus must think something quite different: the more powerful cause can determine the act without affecting the nature, thereby leaving the freedom of the will intact.[28]

As superior cause then, God determines the will to determine itself freely to continue its act of beatific enjoyment. This act would still proceed from the free will, and thus would also be worthy of praise inasmuch as the will still determines itself contingently within its own order.[29] The fact that the blessed do not sin is then preserved by the superior causality of God. It nevertheless remains in the power of the will to sin, but the retention of this remote power does not in any way lessen the happiness of the blessed, because sin never in fact comes about on account of the divine prevenience. All this thus preserves the freedom of the blessed, as long as one allows freedom (as Scotus does) to be retained by an ability which can never in fact be exercised. Langston notes that from the point of view of a libertarian definition of freedom, Scotus's view would hardly be satisfactory. On this view, there is more to freedom than mere ability: one must also have the opportunity to exercise that ability, which the divine prevenience of heaven does not in fact afford. Langston points out that he is not free to swim at his local YMCA on certain nights, because even though he can swim and is a member, those nights are reserved to groups for which he does not qualify. So he is not free to swim on those nights, despite his (remote) ability. On those nights he is not granted the opportunity. Langston in fact takes this argument as evidence against Scotus being a libertarian, despite his reputation as a voluntarist.

[28]   *Ordinatio*, bk 4, dist. 49, q. 6, n. 15 (X, p. 457). See also Langston, *God's Willing Knowledge*, pp. 41–2.
[29]   *Ordinatio*, bk 4, dist. 49, q. 6, n. 15 (X, p. 458).

Someone like Donnelly would no doubt find Scotus unattractive on these grounds. Donnelly himself did indeed see a preventative divine providence at work in heaven. This providence was however one of God's preventing harmful effects resulting from the sins committed there. Donnelly seemed to take it for granted that freedom must allow not only for the continuation of the ability to sin in heaven, but also for the opportunity to sin. Perhaps someone more libertarian still might go further and assert that for true freedom, there must also be the real possibility of one's actions bringing about their proper effects. If someone took this view, even Donnelly's heaven would not be free enough. Our concern, however, is whether someone like Donnelly, if he or she were to abandon heavenly peccability as unorthodox, would then find Scotus's theory attractive, and clearly such a person would not.

Someone like Donnelly would no doubt have little sympathy for Scotus's contention that a metaphysically superior cause can determine an inferior one without infringing on its natural freedom. Donnelly's own account of freedom is certainly inimical to such a notion, though the notion is more easily understandable within an Augustinian medieval framework, in which freedom is seen as something caused by God rather than as set over against him. Not, however, that Scotus's view would have been automatically acceptable to all working within such a framework: Scotus's argument from metaphysical superiority would seem to imply not simply that God could determine the free act of the human will, but that an angel, being superior to a human being, could also accomplish that. Such a position would hardly be acceptable to a St Thomas, for example, who would allow God, though not an angel, to be the cause of human free acts.

So Scotus hardly presents an attractive solution to the problem of heavenly freedom and impeccability. Rather Scotus propounds a theory that attracts objections from various points of view, not just Donnelly's libertarian one.[30] The fact that

---

[30] For a less critical presentation, see Prentice, 'The Degree and Mode of Liberty in the Beatitude of the Blessed', pp. 327–42.

different accounts of freedom have come into view here does suggest that the notion of 'freedom' itself requires further clarification. But before we go further into the notion of freedom, there is a yet more celebrated 'voluntarist' whose doctrine as such deserves the same consideration as Scotus's: another Franciscan friar, William of Ockham.

5

Fruition, Freedom and Indifference: William of Ockham

William of Ockham's doctrine of freedom takes its cue partly from the fact of the moral order. Human actions are praised and blamed, and that implies that they must be free. The will then must have a radical self-determination, so as to be able to be held responsible for its actions.[1] As we shall see, Ockham claims that experience shows us that however much the intellect dictates that something ought to be done, the will still has power to nill it. Though the will is in general inclined to what is pleasurable and away from what is not, towards what is advantageous and just and away from what is not, and can be further inclined by habits, it always retains its superabundant freedom of indifference. Ockham is said to be 'notorious' for this doctrine, according to which the will is radically free.[2]

Whereas Scotus had retained the idea that the 'good' and not evil was the proper object of the will, Ockham allows that the will is free to define the scope of its object, such that it is possible for the will to will evil as such. Although Scotus had denied that the will necessarily willed the ultimate good or happiness with regard to the exercise of the act, he had nevertheless still thought that the will necessarily willed happiness with regard to the act's specification. One could not will to be miserable as such. Not so William of Ockham: however much the will may be inclined in various ways with regard to its object,

[1] See M. M. Adams, 'Ockham on Will, Nature, and Morality', in P. V. Spade (ed.), *The Cambridge Guide to Ockham* (Cambridge: Cambridge University Press, 1999), pp. 245–72.
[2] Adams, 'Ockham on Will, Nature, and Morality', p. 245.

its basic inclination is neutral. Consideration of morality and the will's mastery of its own acts leads Ockham to conclude that human beings must even be able to nill their ultimate good, as we shall see. Like Scotus, Ockham analyses the will's enjoyment of the ultimate end of happiness in both books 1 and 4 of his commentary on Peter Lombard's *Sentences*, on which Ockham had lectured at Oxford early in the fourteenth century. Book 1 of his commentary we have in the form of an *ordinatio* – a text prepared by Ockham himself – and book 4 in the form of a *reportatio* – the uncorrected notes of a student.

Ockham's sixth question of his first book of commentary asks whether the will enjoys its ultimate end *contingently and freely*.[3] Much of it is taken up with disagreement with the details of Scotus's argumentation on 'fruition' or enjoyment, and I shall pass over these. Ockham then presents a number of 'conclusions' concerning the freedom of enjoying one's created beatitude as opposed to one's uncreated beatitude. In Chapter 2, we saw how Suárez was to teach that while the blessed necessarily made an act of love of God, they did not necessarily love their own beatitude with regard to the exercise of the act. It is more with the second of these, the willing of one's (created) beatitude rather than with the willing of the beatific object itself, that Ockham is largely concerned in question 6 of the first book of his commentary.

'Ultimate end', he says, can be taken in two ways. Either it can mean the created beatitude possible for the will, or else it can mean the object of that beatitude. With regard to created beatitude, it is not lawful for the will to 'enjoy' it, strictly speaking. Strictly speaking, it is lawful for the will only to enjoy that beatitude's *object*, and to enjoy anything less is possible but unlawful. However, taking 'enjoyment' or 'fruition' in a broader sense, Ockham gives his view that the will can will, not will, or nill this created beatitude, whether it is manifested in general or in particular, whether on earth or in heaven.[4] Before passing on to what he has to say about the enjoyment of that beatitude's object, I shall review the arguments he puts forward

³   *Ordinatio*, bk 1, q. 6 (*Opera Theologica*, vol. I, pp. 486–507).
⁴   *Ordinatio*, bk 1, q. 6 (I, p. 506).

to support his conclusions, which largely but not exclusively concern created beatitude. In each case he is arguing that beatitude can only be enjoyed freely, in the sense of the freedom of indifference, that freedom which is opposed to necessity rather than merely to compulsion or to slavery to guilt or punishment.[5]

Ockham's first two conclusions are that the will enjoys the 'ultimate end' (conceived either in general or in particular) *freely and contingently*. This is said to be because the will is able both to love created beatitude and not love it, to desire it and not desire it. If the intellect is able to judge that there is no such beatitude, either in particular or in general, nothing in which there is true satisfaction, then beatitude can be nilled.[6] Ockham backs up this reasoning with further points. The first is that when someone wills something knowing its consequences, he or she is able to will those consequences too. Ockham has in mind someone who wills not to be, such as someone who commits suicide or risks death, and such people are found, he says, both among those who believe in an afterlife and those who do not. Given that such people can will not to exist and know that they will consequently not be happy, it is also possible for them to will not to be happy or blessed. Willing not to be happy, they therefore nill happiness or beatitude. The second point is based on those who, while believing that they can obtain beatitude only if they do not sin, nevertheless sin even though they know or believe it will lead to eternal punishment. This can only be, Ockham thinks, because they in fact nill their created beatitude, not only in general but also in particular.

Having established that one can nill beatitude since the intellect can judge the latter impossible, in his third conclusion Ockham adds that beatitude can be nilled even when the intellect judges it possible. While the intellect can judge that created beatitude is not impossible, it can also judge that it will always in fact lack beatitude. Since what the intellect judges can pertain to an act of the will, the will can therefore will always

---

5   *Ordinatio*, bk 1, q. 6 (I, pp. 501–2).
6   *Ordinatio*, bk 1, q. 6 (I, p. 503).

to be without beatitude and thus nill it.[7] Ockham confirms his position by an appeal to further points, the first of which comes from his theology of hell, from what the damned might be able to do if left to themselves. (In the order that in fact obtains, the damned are not left to themselves on Ockham's account, but have their act of will caused by God with their own activity suspended.)[8] If left to themselves, he says, the damned would be able to conform themselves to what they at least believe to be the divine will. However, it is the divine will that they always lack beatitude. Hence the damned would not only judge beatitude not to be something altogether impossible, but might also freely conform themselves to the divine will that they should always lack beatitude. Believing beatitude to be not impossible, they would nevertheless nill it for themselves. If this can be done in hell, Ockham reasons, it can also be done on earth.[9] The second point is based on the premise that whoever wills something efficaciously must also will all they believe to be necessary to obtain what they will. Now a believer believes that beatitude cannot be obtained without a good and holy life but nevertheless might not will to live such a life. Such a believer would hold beatitude to be possible and yet would not efficaciously will it. Hence it is possible not to will beatitude, even when one holds it to be not impossible.

The fourth conclusion passes on from this life to the clear vision of God. Ockham says that someone who saw the divine essence and at the same time were to lack beatific enjoyment or fruition is able to nill that fruition. He proves this from the premise (to which he has already appealed in support of the third conclusion) that the will is able to conform itself to the divine will. Given that God is able to will that one who sees him can always lack beatific fruition, the will in question is able to nill that fruition. A further point is that whatever can be willed or nilled for a time can be willed or nilled for ever. Given that the will can nill beatitude for a determinate time, it can nill it simply for all time.[10]

[7] *Ordinatio*, bk 1, q. 6 (I, p. 504).
[8] *Ordinatio*, bk 1, q. 2 (I, p. 399).
[9] *Ordinatio*, bk 1, q. 6 (I, pp. 504–5).
[10] *Ordinatio*, bk 1, q. 6 (I, p. 505).

The fifth conclusion concerns one who saw the essence of God but who lacked the love of God. Here we are already definitely coming to the question of nilling the *object* of beatitude rather than created beatitude itself, nilling God rather than nilling fruition. Ockham says that his fifth conclusion can be proved or 'persuaded' from the fact that anything 'disadvantageous' (*incommodum*) can be the object of nilling, whether it is in truth disadvantageous or only thought to be such. Now God can at least be thought to be disadvantageous because he punishes the damned. Hence God, clearly seen but not loved, can be nilled.[11] It should be added that for Ockham vision would not entail certainty as to whether or not beatitude and its security would be granted. Elsewhere Ockham says that the 'security' of one's vision comes not from the vision of God itself but by a further act of the blessed distinct from both vision and fruition.[12] Security in beatitude (and hence any knowledge about its perpetuity or otherwise) is not given in the vision of God but only by way of a further act, just as beatitude itself consists formally in the further act of fruition. So, given the lack of such knowledge of security, the one who sees God but does not love him might still view him as possibly disadvantageous. Ockham makes no such points in his commentary, however, but instead brings forward the case of Christ. Christ he holds, along with other medieval theologians, to have been blessed during his life on earth. But even though he was so blessed, Ockham says, he still suffered punishments and sustained bodily penalties. Since such things are disadvantageous, either in the sense that they are so or are simply thought to be so, then God can be disadvantageous in this respect, either in truth or thought. Hence he can be nilled by one who sees his essence but does not love him.[13]

Ockham knows himself to be moving into controversial territory here, and wants to put off further discussion of the freedom or necessity of enjoying God until question 16 of book 4. To the case of nilling *created* happiness Ockham refers his

[11] *Ordinatio*, bk 1, q. 6 (I, pp. 505–6).
[12] *Dubitationes Addititiae*, n. 6 (*Opera Theologica*, VIII, p. 312).
[13] *Ordinatio*, bk 1, q. 6 (I, p. 506).

preceding conclusions.[14] But as for the nilling of its *object*, for now Ockham briefly sets out the following position. On earth God can be the object not only of willing but also of nilling. That is clear enough from what has been said in the preceding conclusions. Moreover, if the beatific object is clearly seen by the intellect, and God were to suspend the will's activity with respect to willing him, God could then be nilled. Again, this is clear enough from the fifth conclusion. He then asks, however, what would be the case if God does *not* suspend the will's activity, but instead were to 'leave it to its own nature'. Is the will then able to make God clearly seen the object of nilling? This is a more doubtful point, he says, making a promise to address the issue in book 4.[15]

The *reportatio* of question 16 of book 4 asks whether the blessed enjoy God *necessarily*.[16] First Ockham puts arguments against this necessity. The will, he says, is the same power in heaven as it was on the journey there, a power that possesses the same manner of acting in regard to all its objects. On earth the will did not enjoy God necessarily, and in heaven it is no different. Moreover, the will just is a rational power which can act with regard to opposites. Hence it can both enjoy God and will the opposite. All good 'voluntarism' so far, until Ockham gives the opposing argument: impeccability. If the beatified will did not enjoy God necessarily and hence could equally well *not* enjoy him, then it would be able to sin. In order then to exclude the possibility of its sinning, the beatified will must enjoy God necessarily after all.[17] Ockham's replies to these opposing arguments are implicit in his own response to the question. However, before he turns to the question itself, he spends time on what exactly enjoyment or fruition is, and whether its possibility for human nature can be established by human reason without the benefit of revelation. On the first of these Ockham is largely concerned to reject the opinion that fruition and 'delight' (*delectatio*) – the latter in fact passive and

14   *Ordinatio*, bk 1, q. 6 (I, pp. 506–7).
15   *Ordinatio*, bk 1, q. 6 (I, p. 507).
16   *Reportatio*, bk 4, q. 16 (VII, pp. 340–61).
17   *Reportatio*, bk 4, q. 16 (VII, p. 340).

concomitant on the act of fruition – are sometimes the same.[18] On the second he rejects some of the arguments reported by Scotus that claimed to demonstrate the possibility of fruition by natural reason.[19]

Ockham only then turns to the main question of whether the blessed enjoy God necessarily. First he repeats and adds to some of his arguments from book 1 on how the 'ultimate end' can be nilled in this life. Beatitude can be judged impossible and so nilled, and is also nilled by those who nill their existence. Ockham emphasises that the will can moreover nill what is judged to be the ultimate end, because the will is a free power open to contrary acts. The will can will and nill with respect to any object, and so can will and nill God.[20] Moreover the will can do the opposite of what right reason dictates, as is clear in this life from experience.[21] He adds that what the will can nill for one individual of the species, it can will for any individual of the species. Thus, just as one can nill beatitude for someone else, so one can nill it for oneself. That the will does not necessarily will the good in general (the general concept of 'good') but can nill it, is shown from the fact that it can be believed that no satisfaction is found in the good *in general*. This conclusion is also said to follow from the fact that the will does not necessarily will any particular good, the movement of the will being the same in regard to both.

Ockham then comes to the clear vision of God. Since the latter could be made to exist without the beatific act of fruition, it is easy to conclude that God is not willed necessarily just because he is seen. That vision can exist without fruition is deduced from the 'rule' that what is prior can be separated from what is posterior.[22] Fruition is subsequent to vision, and so vision can in principle exist alone, and in that case God, though clearly seen, would not be loved and so would not be loved necessarily. The elevation of the will by charity

18 *Reportatio*, bk 4, q. 16 (VII, pp. 341–5).
19 *Reportatio*, bk 4, q. 16 (VII, pp. 345–9).
20 *Reportatio*, bk 4, q. 16 (VII, p. 350).
21 *Reportatio*, bk 4, q. 16 (VII, pp. 350–1).
22 On this rule, see M. M. Adams, *William Ockham* (Notre Dame, IN: University of Notre Dame Press, 1987), vol. 2, pp. 1253–4.

(or some other habit that does not remove the use of reason) is also unable to necessitate a beatific act of the will. Such an elevated will can still nill beatitude.[23] Ockham's proof is one also used in book 1 with regard to one who sees God but lacks fruition, and is based on the premise that everything which can be the object of the will for a time can be such an object for all time. Since beatitude can be nilled for a time by way of mortal sin, therefore it can be so nilled for all time in this life and thus also in heaven.[24] Ockham then uses yet another argument familiar from book 1, this time based on the principle that every will can conform itself to a divine precept. Since God, he says, can command that the created will hate him, the created will can do that and thus nill him. Ockham then adds that if an action can be right in this life, it can also be right in the next. Since God could make it right to hate him in this life by commanding it, so the same can be the case in heaven.

Now we come to the case of one who is truly blessed, that is, not one who just sees God, but one who also makes the beatific act of the will, namely, fruition or enjoyment. Ockham declares that it can be said that one who sees God clearly, and has his beatific act 'entirely' (*totaliter*) caused by God, cannot nill God. The acts of loving and hating formally exclude one another, so one cannot both will and nill God.[25] However, this is all based on the beatific act being entirely or totally caused by God. In this case it would seem that God *is* necessarily enjoyed, though not because he is seen but because the act of willing is 'entirely' caused by God. Ockham holds that in most cases God and creatures act together as 'partial' causes. God does not will to produce most effects alone, but acts as a partial cause together with a created secondary cause, such that the partial causality exercised by the secondary cause is not superfluous.[26] Here, however, God suspends the causal power of the secondary cause (that is, the beatified will) and acts as the total efficient

---

[23]   *Reportatio*, bk 4, q. 16 (VII, p. 351).
[24]   *Reportatio*, bk 4, q. 16 (VII, pp. 351–2).
[25]   *Reportatio*, bk 4, q. 16 (VII, p. 352).
[26]   *Reportatio*, bk 2, qq. 3–4 (V, p. 72). See also Adams, *William Ockham*, pp. 1228–31.

cause of the will's enjoyment. The beatific act then will not be a free but a necessary act.[27]

Ockham then goes on immediately to ask what would be the case if the beatific act were *not* totally caused by God, if the will were 'left entirely to its own nature and freedom' (*reliqueretur totaliter naturae suae et libertati*). So if God were to suspend beatific fruition on this scenario, then the will would be *free* to will God. Such an act of willing would not be truly beatific, Ockham thinks, because, if it were, it would be in the power of the blessed freely to become both blessed and wretched as they pleased, which Ockham rejects. Such a will would be not only free to will him but also free *not* to will him and so also to nill him. If God were to suspend the activity of the will with respect to volition, then the will could nill God.[28] That it could do so is confirmed by the fact that a power naturally inclined to something receives the contrary only with violence to its nature. But there is no violence when a will nills God, demonstrating that there is no natural inclination to will God and not nill him.[29]

At this point in the text, according to its editors, the argument becomes 'incomplete and confused'.[30] It seems to me that Ockham is now responding to the suggestion that the will left to itself would nevertheless still will God *necessarily* on account of the fact that the intellect, seeing God clearly, judges that he can only be willed and not nilled. So, on this suggestion, seeing God clearly, one judges that God cannot be nilled but only willed, and the will must conform its act to intellect's judgement. The critical edition, however, speaks of the blessed judging that God is to be *nilled* and in no way *willed*: *beatus iudicat Deum esse nolendum et nullo modo volendum*. Some manuscripts, however, reverse nilling and willing, reading *beatus iudicat Deum esse volendum et nullo modo nolendum*. So, according to the critical edition, the blessed here judge that God must be nilled and in no way willed, but according to some manuscripts, they judge that God must be willed and in no way nilled. I

27   Cf. *Reportatio*, bk 2, q. 15 (VII, pp. 355–6).
28   *Reportatio*, bk 4, q. 16 (VII, p. 352).
29   *Reportatio*, bk 4, q. 16 (VII, pp. 352–3).
30   *Reportatio*, bk 4, q. 16 (VII, p. 353, n. 1).

suggest that while the critical edition may correctly identify what the reporting student wrote down, the other reading corrects that report to what Ockham almost certainly said. It represents the very position against which Ockham wants to argue.

This position then states that the will, left to its own freedom, wills God necessarily on account of its judgement that God can only be willed and not nilled, a judgement to which the will must conform. Ockham finds two problems with this position. However, these do not include the objection that the intellect could not make such a judgement on the ground that it is erroneous. It *is* erroneous, according to Ockham, because God *can* be nilled after all. Nevertheless, he first acknowledges that the intellect *could* make such an erroneous judgement. The judgement is erroneous, because God *can* be nilled, but it is possible to *make* such an erroneous judgement, because such erroneous judgements can be made about things other than God. The intellect can judge erroneously then that other objects are to 'be willed and in no way nilled'. Since such erroneous judgements can be made with regard to other objects, they can also be made with regard to God.

The first of Ockham's objections to the position in question is that it implies that the will must necessarily conform to all the judgements of the intellect. Ockham rejects this, since the consequence would be that no act would ever be meritorious or otherwise, since no act would remain in the power of the will. So Ockham allows that the will, when left to itself, can always not submit to the intellect's judgement. The second objection is that the will is no more necessitated with regard to any object whatsoever than it is with regard to what is impossible. But since the will is not necessitated but free to will and nill the impossible, in just the same way is it free to will and nill whatever other object it pleases.[31]

Ockham's own position then is that, if God left the will to its own freedom, it would will God not necessarily but *freely* (and therefore would also be able to nill him), but if God himself caused its act totally, God would instead be willed *necessarily*

---

[31]   *Reportatio*, bk 4, q. 16 (VII, p. 353).

(and the will rendered unable to do anything other). Next Ockham answers a query as to whether one perfectly blessed could nill what God wills. He replies by denying that they can: willing God in this way formally excludes nilling what he wills. The blessed will and love God and anything he wills and loves. If such a one nilled what God willed, he would be at the same time both willing and nilling the same thing, and that is impossible.[32] We can see then how an account of impeccability follows on from the fact that God is the total cause of the act of fruition. Given God's total causality, the will can do no other than enjoy God, and that formally excludes both nilling God and nilling what he wills. Hence the original argument in favour of the necessity of the act of fruition – that it must be so if the saints are to be impeccable – holds, once one assumes the total causality of God.

What then would Ockham's solution have to say to the original arguments against the necessity of fruition and in favour of its freedom? These arguments were good 'voluntarist' objections, arguing from the freedom of indifference. Ockham of course would concede that the will remains able to nill God, *if* left to its own nature and freedom. What in fact happens in heaven is that the will is *not* left to its own freedom, but its beatific act is totally caused by God. This would of course seem to remove the blessed's freedom, but Ockham seems unwilling to concede that they are simply unfree. This matter is partly treated among various doubts which arise from his solution. It is not the only doubt: another is Aristotle's *dictum* that the wicked are always ignorant.[33] Ockham's solution of course rejects the idea that ignorance must be presupposed to the nilling of God. Ockham allows that even with the clear vision of God, the latter can still be nilled, where the will is left to its own freedom. So Ockham presents his own interpretation of the connection between ignorance and evil: if one acts in an evil rather than a good way, then one will be ignorant of what one would have learned had one acted

<hr/>

[32] *Reportatio*, bk 4, q. 16 (VII, pp. 353–4).
[33] *Reportatio*, bk 4, q. 16 (VII, p. 354). Cf. Aristotle, *Nicomachean Ethics*, bk 3, ch. 1 (1110b 28–30; ET: pp. 120–1).

well.[34] The first of the *dubia*, however, concerns the nature of freedom itself.

The first doubt is that indifference seems to be no longer part of the very notion of freedom. (As we have already seen, Ockham is 'notorious' for defining freedom in terms of indifference.) Ockham quotes Anselm's teaching that the ability to sin is neither freedom nor part of it. But then it would seem that if it is through indifference that one can sin, then indifference is not going to be part of freedom.[35] Now Ockham is prepared to concede what Anselm says about the ability to sin not being part of freedom, because he does not wish it to be implied that either God or the blessed could sin. He does not wish it to be the case that saying a subject is free entails saying that that subject could sin. Ockham wants to say that both God and the blessed are free, but at the same time does not want that to imply that they are able to sin. So he concedes to Anselm that peccability is no part of freedom. Freedom and the ability to sin are related to one another as follows: whoever can sin has freedom, but not all who have freedom can sin. One who can sin has freedom with respect to those acts that are sinful, but neither God nor the blessed have freedom with respect to sinful acts but only with respect to those that are not sinful.

So while God is free, he nevertheless cannot sin. He still has a freedom of indifference, but this indifference is not with respect to acts which can be described as sinful. At first this sounds as though Ockham is placing a limit on the divine freedom of indifference: certain acts are ruled out for him, because he cannot sin. However, Ockham asserts that God can cause everything positive in an act of sin. What he does not want is for this to imply that God is himself sinning when he does this. Now in Ockham's view, God would have sinned in this, had he been obliged to cause the opposite of the sin, just as the creature is obliged to cause the opposite and not sin. God, however, has no obligations. So he can cause the very same sinful acts that creatures may cause, and yet for him they

[34] *Reportatio*, bk 4, q. 16 (VII, pp. 357–8).
[35] *Reportatio*, bk 4, q. 16 (VII, p. 354). See Anselm, *De Libertate Arbitrii*, ch. 1 (I, pp. 207–9; ET: pp. 175–6).

are not sins because he was not obliged to do the opposite. This means that God's freedom of indifference does not have its scope lessened by the fact that he cannot sin. He can still cause all possible actions which are sinful, but he does not sin in doing so.[36] Hence, in respect of God, Ockham can accept Anselm's saying that the ability to sin is not part of freedom.

Ockham only explicitly justifies his position here with regard to God. But he also wants to maintain that the blessed are free and are yet impeccable. He states that the blessed, like God, retain their freedom of indifference with regard to those acts which are not sinful. So they are free to do what is good but not what is evil. How though can Ockham do this without seeing the possible objects of their indifference reduced, and thus their freedom reduced? While he has managed not to reduce the scope of God's possible actions by an appeal to the fact that God has no obligations, he cannot plausibly do the same with regard to the blessed, since they are still subject to God's will and therefore to obligations. To be the cause of sinful actions would not make God a sinner, but would nevertheless still make the blessed into sinners.

Ockham is not however concerned to defend himself against the accusation that the freedom of the blessed has been reduced. He only wants to show that they are still free even though they are impeccable. Had he wanted to argue that they were *more* free, he might have appealed to the freedom from slavery to punishment and guilt. In book 1 he had distinguished the freedom of indifference from this freedom, and there asserted that in terms of freedom from servitude the blessed were more free.[37] However, perhaps Ockham (like Suárez) would have seen that as mere equivocation at this point. Moreover, when treating of angels in the second book, Ockham directly states that, though the blessed are more free in terms of freedom from servitude, in terms of the freedom of indifference 'wayfarers' or 'pilgrims' are freer than those who have arrived in heaven. The reason for this is that God's total causality has intervened,

---

[36]   *Reportatio*, bk 4, q. 16 (VII, p. 355). On this in relation to omnipotence, see Adams, *William Ockham*, pp. 1160–2.
[37]   *Ordinatio*, bk 1, q. 6 (I, p. 501).

suspending the free activity of the beatified will in this respect.[38] So while Ockham maintains that the blessed are truly free in respect of non-sinful acts, he concedes that they are nevertheless *less free* than they were on earth on account of their heavenly impeccability.

We turned our attention to William of Ockham in order to see whether a true 'voluntarist' who also embraced heavenly impeccability might offer a theory persuasive to someone like Donnelly, who, if persuaded to accept the orthodoxy of impeccability, would still wish to protect the freedom of the beatified will as far as possible. Having turned already to another celebrated voluntarist, Duns Scotus, and found him wanting, we turned to Ockham as a yet more notorious promoter of the freedom of indifference, someone we might presume to be even more likely to maintain freedom as much as possible in an impeccable heaven. And indeed, while Scotus allowed the blessed a remote freedom to sin by refraining from willing God (but not nilling him, since that would be impossible), Ockham allows the blessed even to nill God, if left to their own freedom. Ockham, however, as a way of maintaining impeccability (since that is Christian orthodoxy), has the activity of the wills of the blessed suspended. In contrast, Scotus had not wanted to have the free nature of the blessed overridden in this respect, and had asserted that, as a metaphysically superior cause, God could determine that the beatific act of will was freely continued by the blessed. Ockham, however, has removed the beatific act from the blessed will altogether and made God its total cause. It seems that the more voluntarist a theologian becomes, the more he must perhaps limit the freedom of the blessed in order to maintain an orthodox position on impeccability. In the final analysis, despite being a greater promoter of indifference, Ockham seems to present a picture of heavenly freedom even less attractive to someone like Donnelly than Scotus does, because Ockham ends up with a radical suppression of freedom with respect to beatitude. It seems that the greater a promoter of the freedom of indifference one is, the more one must either suppress freedom in this

---

[38] *Reportatio*, bk 2, q. 15 (V, pp. 355–6).

respect, like Ockham, or suppress impeccability, as Donnelly had done.

So perhaps a more attractive orthodox theology of heavenly impeccability might lie not so much in suppressing freedom as in a more careful examination of what exactly freedom is. We have seen that one possible response to the charge that freedom is suppressed in heaven is to assert that freedom is in fact maintained or even perfected there. But that was to court the further charge of equivocation, or at least it would seem to invite such a charge in all fairness if a new meaning of freedom were introduced simply as an ad hoc solution to a particular problem, while leaving the old meaning of freedom operative more generally. It is surely no real solution simply to change the meaning of the word 'freedom' when one runs into difficulties with it. What is required is something more than the sudden introduction of a new meaning of freedom as an ad hoc solution to a particular problem. So a theory of heavenly impeccability, which maintains heavenly freedom, would surely be more persuasive, if it were based on a more careful examination of the broader issues involved in freedom and not simply on those raised by the theology of heaven. And so we turn in the next chapter from freedom in eschatology to freedom in moral theory.

6

Two Freedoms, Two Moral Systems

If the blessed are impeccable, does their inability to sin destroy their freedom? In response to this worry, Donnelly suggested that the orthodox Christian view of heaven made room for sin and in this way protected human freedom. Given that Donnelly's view is in fact untenable when judged according to its orthodoxy, I have examined the theories of impeccability propounded by two celebrated Christian 'voluntarists' who might as such be expected to preserve a very great place for freedom in heaven, but found both of them wanting in different ways. Another avenue of enquiry, however, is suggested by some of those to whom Rod Liddle put his question: 'Is there free will in heaven?' As I said in Chapter 1, Liddle found that some of his respondents 'quibbled' over the meaning of free will. But perhaps their concern about the definition of 'free will' was more than mere quibbling. After all, in the course of the last five chapters it has become apparent that the meaning of 'freedom' and 'free will' is by no means obvious. As a way forward, I propose in this chapter to give an account of a divergence between two traditions regarding freedom identified by the twentieth-century moral theologian, Fr Servais Pinckaers OP.[1] I shall then apply his conclusions in the field of Catholic moral theology to that of eschatology. We shall then be able to find out whether the results of this procedure can clarify what

---

[1] *The Sources of Christian Ethics* (Edinburgh: T&T Clark, 1995). *Sources* is a translation by Sr Mary Thomas Noble OP of the third edition of *Les sources de la morale chrétienne* (Fribourg: University Press, 1993).

might be meant when we ask whether free will is excluded from heaven by the inability to sin.

For Pinckaers, the concept of freedom is one of the 'first foundations' of the edifice of moral theology.[2] In his search for a more adequate definition of freedom, Pinckaers makes use of the method not only of reflection on the individual's actions but also of reflection on moral systems. This means an examination of how moral systems are developed and structured from the perspective of a certain concept of freedom. Pinckaers identifies 'two main broad types of organisation of moral material' in the history of Catholic theology. One, characteristic of the Fathers and the 'great scholastic period' (meaning chiefly St Thomas Aquinas), is based on the question of happiness (beatitude) and the virtues; the other, characteristic of the 'modern era', is dominated by theories of obligation and commandments. Pinckaers says that, in each case, tracing the internal logic of these systems will lead to a distinctive concept of freedom. The root of the obligation theory is the 'freedom of indifference' (which we have already been encountering in previous chapters), while the root of the happiness and virtue theory is what he calls 'freedom for excellence' (*liberté de qualité*). Two different concepts of freedom give rise to two different theories of morality.[3]

We have already met the obligation theory in Chapter 2, in connection with Suárez. There I recorded Mahoney's impression of Suárez as preserving a field of action for the freedom of indifference in the face of the claims of the law. I also suggested that Suárez faced the same challenge in his eschatology: marking out a place for freedom in the face of heavenly necessity and obligation. Pinckaers is more concerned, however, with the role of William of Ockham. The 'crucial and decisive moment' came historically, Pinckaers says, when Ockham worked out his particular theology of freedom.[4] According to Pinckaers, Ockham was the initiator of a certain concept of freedom widely adopted by theologians and philosophers after him. This meant

---

[2]   *Sources*, p. 327.
[3]   *Sources*, pp. 328–9.
[4]   *Sources*, p. 329.

that the freedom of indifference came to the fore with morality conceived in terms of obligation and precept, and Pinckaers reports that the freedom of indifference remains 'the most widespread concept today'.[5] So we can recognise in Suárez's view of freedom and morality a successor to Ockham's theories. Moreover, we can already recognise in Wall and Donnelly the continuing widespread influence of indifference, and to this I shall return. Pinckaers's purpose, however, is to bring to the fore once more the other concept of freedom, 'freedom for excellence', which he judges to be 'richer and more adequate' than indifference.[6]

Pinckaers finds in Ockham (and earlier Franciscan tradition) a radical primacy of free will. Being so fundamental, there were no prior principles from which freedom could be demonstrated: it was postulated as a first fact of human experience. Freedom lay in the power of the will to choose between contraries, a power that resided in the will alone.[7] 'It was the power to opt for the yes or the no, to choose between what reason dictated and its contrary, between willing and not willing, acting and not acting, between what the law prescribed and its contrary.'[8] Pinckaers notes that the will was no longer defined as an attraction for the good, exercised in love and desire (as the Fathers and St Thomas had understood it), but the will was practically identified with the freedom of indifference. We are familiar enough from the last chapter with the nature and extent of Ockham's understanding of freedom: even one who has the vision of God, if left to his or her freedom, can nill God and happiness. There I also recorded how Ockham's views are very much aiming to preserve the reality of human morality. Pinckaers, however, sees Ockham as in fact demolishing the richer moral theory taught by St Thomas.[9]

Pinckaers characterises Ockham's 'breach' between freedom and one's 'natural inclinations' as his decisive move. Instead of men and women being naturally and ineluctably disposed

5   *Sources*, p. 330.
6   *Sources*, p. 329.
7   *Sources*, pp. 329–32.
8   *Sources*, p. 332.
9   *Sources*, p. 338.

towards beatitude, being so ordered is now subject to a contingent choice of freedom. Natural inclinations are therefore not so much part of the essential core of human freedom as something below it, placed on a lower plane. Modern moral theories based on the freedom of indifference thus come to create a 'profound opposition' between freedom and natural inclinations, the latter threatening the former with their interior influence on the human person. This Pinckaers identifies as the origin of the divorce between moral theory and the desire for happiness that he finds in his own time. A break had thus been effected with the thinking of the ancient philosophers, as well as of Christian thinking through the Fathers to St Thomas himself.[10]

Pinckaers says that it should be no surprise that such a rupture and revolution in the human soul should result in an upheaval in all moral ideas and in their systematic organisation. Instead of the passions or emotions (which he refers to as 'sensibility') being regarded as able to be good and possessing a positive moral value, they are seen as a threat to freedom. Freedom best asserted itself in a struggle against emotion and not just against passion's excess. Moreover, instead of the virtues bringing the natural inclinations to perfection as a second nature, such habits, as stable principles of action, now stand in tension with the essential indeterminacy of freedom. The stronger the habit, the more freedom's scope was reduced and the free quality of actions diminished. 'Virtue' ceases to be part of freedom and loses its central place in moral theory, becoming more or less a convenient category for the listing of moral obligations.[11]

Furthermore, the break between freedom and natural inclinations and the virtues sundered any pattern of continuity between the moral life and its goal, in which human acts were linked in an organic whole within the perspective of final beatitude. Given that freedom consisted entirely in a choice between contraries, each action was cut off from all those preceding and following it. According to Pinckaers, past actions

---

[10]   *Sources*, pp. 332–5.
[11]   *Sources*, pp. 335–6.

could not be allowed to threaten freedom by determining any future actions, and so each action was isolated as an 'atom', severed from any continuity of a wider moral life. If sometimes hampered by external forces, freedom of indifference was nevertheless always a given, and hence had no need of real growth to any maturity. Moral theory would focus itself on such isolated individual actions, and individual cases of conscience would become the stuff of modern moral theology.[12]

Finally, there is a 'shift in loyalties'. Loyalty now becomes a threat to freedom, because it is a *bond* between the will and some good, an ideal, a person, a way of life, an institution or a previous choice. Such a permanence in the will can only be conceived as a threat to freedom, because it is detrimental to the freedom to choose between contraries. Betrayal then becomes the good which leaves the field open to the passion of self-affirmation, of loyalty only to self, and the normal faithfulness required for living in society becomes mere repetition of the same or similar atomic choices. This rupture between freedom and loyalty joins the other ruptures of freedom from natural inclinations and sensibility, habits and virtues, finality and continuity, to meet in the 'final break' that takes place between free will and reason itself.[13]

Again we have already seen in Chapter 5 how far Ockham went in granting the will independence from the intellect, setting freedom firmly in this autonomous will. The power to say no to the intellect was no weakness in freedom but was rather of its very essence. Subsequent moral theology became divided between rationalists and voluntarists, as each faculty was seen as independent of and in tension with the other. However, since morality was seen as residing in the domain of freedom and therefore pertaining to the will, moral theology became focused on law, commandments and obedience, with the rational content of precepts marginalised and the role of reason increasingly limited to discovering whether or nor a binding precept existed that was relevant to the moral case under discussion. Law itself was considered less as an ordination of

[12] *Sources*, pp. 336–8.
[13] *Sources*, p. 340.

reason for the common good, as St Thomas had understood it, and more as proceeding merely from the free will of God. According to Pinckaers, human freedom and divine freedom were thus both fixed, and fixed in radical isolation, 'indifferent' to one another. Moral theology was marked by an 'irreducible' tension between human freedom and the legal obligation which limited and constrained it. The content of the moral law rested so much on the will of God, who was free, absolutely speaking, to command that a human being hate him. For Ockham, this did not exclude human beings coming to know through conscience and revelation what God had in fact ordained, but the role of reason had been seriously reduced from the position it had previously held.[14]

Pinckaers asserts that in these and other ways, 'freedom of indifference' influenced all western thought, even where its name was not known, remaining not simply on the level of ideas and doctrines but penetrating life and its deepest experiences. Pinckaers takes as a sure sign of the presence of this freedom various tensions or disconnections, such as between freedom and law, freedom and reason, freedom and nature, freedom and grace, divine and human freedom, subject and object, freedom and sensibility, my freedom and the freedom of others, the individual and society. The tension between them was expressed in an 'either ... or' formula, of which I shall give some of Pinckaers's examples: either a moral action pertained to the law or it pertained to freedom; something pertained to freedom or reason, reason engendering a determinism that opposed voluntary choice; something pertained to freedom or nature, freedom as non-nature seeking to dominate and exploit irrational and blind nature; either grace or freedom: what was ascribed to divine grace became difficult to ascribe to human freedom and vice versa; either God was free or human beings were: the one could not be exalted without the other's diminishment; either my freedom or that of others: the freedom of others becomes a threat to my own, and the individual is set also against society, with the bonds between individuals severed, leaving them mere atoms and society only

[14] *Sources*, pp. 340–9.

an artificial creation and restraint. Thus proceeds modern thinking and life under the influence of the freedom of indifference.[15]

In the next chapter, I shall argue that Donnelly's eschatology is in essence a thoroughgoing application of the freedom of indifference to the theology of the last things, one so thoroughgoing that the last things are hardly 'last' at all. I shall also note some of the consequences of the freedom of indifference for the eschatologies of the other theologians I have considered so far. The remainder of this chapter, however, will be devoted to a presentation of Pinckaers's alternative to freedom of indifference in moral theology, namely, his 'freedom for excellence'. Then in the next chapter I shall be able to apply fully both what Pinckaers has to say about freedom of indifference and what he has to say about freedom for excellence to the theology of heaven, and in particular to the problem of freedom and impeccability.

Pinckaers begins with certain examples of exterior actions in the arts. With the help of these examples, one of a child learning to play the piano and the other of someone learning a foreign language, he intends to discern the freedom at work in more interior moral actions. To play the piano, a child must first have certain predispositions (such as an attraction to music and an ear for it) without which anything more would be a waste of time. With the help of a teacher and regular exercises, a gifted child can then learn the rules of this art and develop his or her talent. Though lessons and practice may be experienced as something of a constraint imposed on 'freedom and the attractions of the moment', with effort and perseverance the child will progress and play with accuracy, rhythm and a certain ease, even in more difficult pieces. As talent and taste develop, the child will play in a more 'personal' way and even delight in improvising. A truly gifted child may graduate yet further as an artist or composer. Pinckaers intends this example to show how the one who has acquired this art has acquired a new freedom, a musical freedom in his or her ability to play whatever he or she chooses and even to compose new pieces. Pinckaers defines this musical freedom of the child as 'the gradually acquired ability to execute works of his desire with perfection': it is a 'habit' based on natural dispositions and developed and stabilised by regular, progressive exercises.[16]

Pinckaers's second example follows the same pattern. To speak a foreign language, a minimum predisposition is first required, followed by perseverance in following the rules of the language, as one takes courses and visits the place where the language is spoken. Gradual improvement will lead to ease and enjoyment in speaking the language. A new freedom, subject to the constraints of grammatical rules, will be found in which one is free to choose words to form sentences of one's choice. Pinckaers says that this freedom is not to be confused with a freedom to make mistakes. Instead this linguistic freedom lies in the ability to *avoid* making mistakes without the need for conscious effort in doing so. This is a freedom for excellence, because it enables one to speak and understand with perfection.[17] I should add that Pinckaers might also have made the same distinction between the freedom for excellence and the freedom to make mistakes in his first example. There the musical freedom attained enables one to play well with ease, to avoid making mistakes without the constant conscious effort to do so. In the first example too, we can distinguish between the freedom for excellence and the freedom to commit faults.

Pinckaers now moves from examples in the arts to an example in the moral order. Of the many virtues he could choose, Pinckaers selects the virtue of courage. He gives an account of its development as progressive and acquired through small, repeated victories of self-conquest. It grows with 'dogged effort' to render a service, overcome laziness, or whatever, and is learned through example, discipline and the encouragement of others. This virtue is characteristic of a morally mature person and is indispensable, Pinckaers says, to complete moral freedom. Once acquired, it enables one to take on projects of high value despite internal and external resistance, obstacles, and opposition. The person without such courage might boast

[16]   *Sources*, pp. 354–5.
[17]   *Sources*, pp. 355–6.

of their freedom to break rules and so on, but would in fact be weak in freedom because he or she would not know how to form a lasting determination strong enough to deal with the pressure of circumstances or feelings.[18] This 'courageous freedom' is thus very different from the freedom of indifference. The acquiring of the habit again leads to a new freedom for excellence, which we might contrast with the freedom to fail in this regard.

In contrast to the tension between natural inclinations and the freedom of indifference, Pinckaers emphasises that the freedom for excellence presupposes natural inclinations, is rooted in them and draws strength from them. In contrast to the arts, here all people possess basic moral inclinations and a primal moral sense. The natural root of the freedom for excellence develops principally through a sense of the true and the good, of uprightness and love, and a desire for knowledge and happiness. Natural inclinations are thus not a lessening of freedom but its very foundation. The more they are developed, the freer a human being becomes. Freedom is characterised here not by indifference, but by a spontaneous attraction to all that at least seems to be true and good. The morality based on this freedom will thus be one of attraction rather than obligation.[19]

Freedom can however be enslaved by weaknesses and faults, and so experience shows up the need for education at the moral level, just as in the world of art. While freedom of indifference admitted of no growth or degrees, freedom for excellence requires the slow, patient work of moral education for its gradual development. To this education Pinckaers assigns three basic stages, which I shall only briefly indicate here. First there is the stage of discipline, in which the rules of the moral law are presented to a child. The child needs to learn that though these rules may be experienced as a limitation on freedom to do what one pleases, their purpose is in fact to help develop his or her ability to perform actions of real excellence by removing dangerous excesses and guarding against unhealthy errors.[20]

[18] *Sources*, pp. 356–7.
[19] *Sources*, pp. 357–9.
[20] *Sources*, pp. 359–63.

The second stage is characterised by the taking of one's own moral life in hand in the development of the virtues.[21] The third stage is where freedom is brought to mature adulthood in the 'mastery of excellent actions and creative fruitfulness'.[22] This self-mastery draws together all one's faculties, desires and feelings, and directs them all to the higher end one is pursuing. Rather than the will remaining ultimately separated from other faculties and the individual's freedom separated from other freedoms (as with indifference), this freedom is open to the contribution of all the other powers to action, and to collaboration with others for the common good and growth of society.

So while freedom for excellence may be contrasted with the freedom of indifference by its rootedness in the natural inclinations for the good and the true, it also has an essential need for development and growth to this maturity, while freedom of indifference was always whole and entire. Moreover, while freedom of indifference was entire in each independent isolated act of freedom, freedom for excellence integrates actions in view of an end, which unites them interiorly and ensures continuity. Growth and a certain pattern of continuity in view of an end characterise freedom for excellence in a way lacking to the freedom of indifference. Virtues now become not something for which freedom has no need (as with the freedom of indifference) but something essential to freedom, being required for that development which is of its very essence. While law was seen by freedom of indifference as an external restraint and a limitation of freedom in irreducible tension with it, it is now seen as a necessary external aid to the development of freedom, together with the inner attraction to the true and the good. The development of the virtues interiorise this law as they progressively develop one's basic inclination to the true and the good. Freedom for excellence thus gives rise to a moral theory of attraction to the good very different from the one of command and obligation based on the freedom of indifference.[23]

---

[21]   *Sources*, pp. 363–6.
[22]   *Sources*, p. 366.
[23]   *Sources*, p. 375.

Pinckaers evidently favours the morality of excellence as a richer moral theory than that of indifference, obligation and precept. He also holds that freedom for excellence is in greater conformity with Scripture, and harmonises well with the moral theories of happiness and virtue found in the ancient world and among the Fathers and in the works of Thomas Aquinas.[24] Pinckaers spends some time verifying his claim that the writings of St Thomas agree with 'freedom for excellence'. In these writings Pinckaers finds all the principal characteristics that he has claimed mark out this freedom. Freedom, for Aquinas, is rooted in the natural inclination of intellect and will to the highest truth and goodness. Founded in the universality of truth and goodness, free will's objects are the ways and means that lead us to our end, while the ultimate end itself (beatitude) does not fall under those things which are a matter of choice. In this way freedom is entirely orientated towards finality, our ultimate happiness, although it can swerve away from its proper goal, though that is not a property which is essential to freedom as such. Aquinas's moral teaching is thus one based on the ultimate end of human beings, an end which unifies human action. His focus is therefore not so much on obligation, commandments and sin as on happiness, choice (arising from the intimate collaboration of will and intellect) and the virtues (which develop one's natural inclinations to truth and goodness). Such a moral theory arises from Thomas's commitment to the freedom for excellence, says Pinckaers.[25]

In the course of his verification of the assertion that Thomas endorses 'freedom for excellence', Pinckaers raises what he says looks like the 'main objection' to the Thomist theory of freedom. Thomas allows that a human being is free in regard to all particular goods, because of the fact that the intellect and will were open to the *universal* good. The problem is that this seems to imply that if the intellect grasped something purely good in itself with no limit or imperfection, that object would so answer to the longing of the will for the good, that the will would no longer be free with regard to it.[26] Indeed, as we have already

[24] *Sources*, pp. 377–8.
[25] *Sources*, pp. 379–99.
[26] *Sources*, p. 394.

seen, St Thomas admits that one wills happiness or beatitude of necessity: one cannot will not to be blessed or to be wretched. Such necessity follows from the fact of the very basis of freedom, Pinckaers says, the fact that the will is naturally inclined to the good. Pinckaers asks, however, whether this situation imposes a choice between freedom and its foundation, and adds that this difficulty could be compounded by a manifestation of God through revelation, since God is himself the universal good, as philosophy can also discover: Would not a person placed before God in this way lose his or her freedom?[27]

Pinckaers presents St Thomas's response to the problem with the help of those texts where he speaks of a distinction between necessity in terms of specification and necessity in terms of exercise.[28] We have already encountered this distinction in Chapter 2 with respect to Suárez, and then in Chapter 3, where I applied it to Duns Scotus. Pinckaers gives St Thomas's view that if the will apprehended a good in which there were all possible goods, the will would necessarily be moved by it according to the specification of the action, because it could not will the contrary. This means that one could not hate such a good. However, in terms of the exercise of the act, it is not the case that this object is willed necessarily, because one could will not to think about happiness. This freedom rests on the will's ability to turn the intellect away from something it could not however will against.[29] As I said above, we have seen this distinction at work in those theologians already considered. Suárez applied it to our created beatitude in heaven, saying that we need not necessarily be thinking about our happiness, but we could never will against it. Scotus, as we have seen, applied something like the distinction to the blessed willing God himself: we are not free to reject God (nill him) but we can in principle turn our wills to something else (not will him) even though God in fact prevents that from happening.

It has been a matter of debate, however, as to whether St Thomas, though he agrees that in terms of the *exercise* of the act

---

[27] *Sources*, p. 395.
[28] The main text is *De Malo*, q. 6, a. un. (XXIII, pp. 145–53; ET: pp. 551–64). Cf. *Summa Theologiae*, 1a.2ae., q. 10, a. 2 (XVII, pp. 86–91).
[29] *Sources*, pp. 395–6.

we need not think about 'happiness' and so are free, also thinks that we still remain free in terms of the exercise of the act when faced with the essence of God, who himself contains every good and is without any lack or imperfection. In other words, do the texts in which St Thomas said that our will was necessitated by the ultimate good according to specification but not according to *exercise*, apply to the beatific vision in the next life as well as our thoughts about happiness in this life, or do these texts apply only to this life and not the next? As we saw in Chapter 2, Suárez thought that these texts applied to the next life as well as to this. So, on Suárez's interpretation, Thomas thought that while the blessed could not nill God (being necessitated to will him in terms of specification), they could still just not will him (not being necessitated in terms of exercise). Taking Thomas in this way, Suárez rejected his view, thinking instead that in heaven the blessed were in fact necessitated in terms of exercise as well as specification. Other more 'Thomist' commentators on St Thomas, however, took a different view. They thought that these texts applied only to the present life, so that while one was free with regard to the exercise of the act in this life (and could stop thinking about beatitude), one was not so free in the next with regard to God himself when seen as he really is. So these commentators agreed with Suárez as to the truth of what really happened in heaven, but while they supposed that St Thomas had also got it right, Suárez thought Thomas had got it wrong. The interpretation of Thomas popular among the more Thomist commentators has remained with us: to the relevant text in the Blackfriars edition of the *Summa*, Fr Thomas Gilby OP adds the footnote: 'No object in our present life [necessitates the will with regard to exercise] . . . nothing could restrain our love were God seen face to face.'[30]

So where does Pinckaers stand in this difference of interpretation? The matter is clearly of some interest, since Pinckaers refers to the passages in question precisely with the intention of rebutting the charge that according to St Thomas the perfect good necessitates our will and removes our freedom. It appears that Pinckaers takes the view of his Thomist predecessors. He

[30] Blackfriars edn., vol. XVII, p. 89, n. c.

speaks of the will from its subjective viewpoint being able to set limits on the intellect's consideration of happiness and the perfect good. In this is its 'escape, so to speak, from the grasp of the perfect good'. The good can present itself as the most attractive, most noble reality in itself, but the effort to grasp it required on our part, and the possible pain involved, can place limitations on even the most perfect good. Some considerable effort is required, because the entire personality is engaged; what is most painful is also required, because we must go out of ourselves and surrender to the good. What is most attractive is also most painful for us, because of its demands, and sin holds us back.[31] All this, however, is concerned only with this world and not the next, where this good is seen face to face without the difficulties of the present life. Pinckaers does not go so far as to say that we can elude the highest good in heaven, and the logic of his Thomist position is that we cannot. So while he may have defended our freedom in terms of our freedom of exercise on earth, his use of these passages does nothing to defend Thomas from the charge that he has us lose our freedom in the beatific vision. Pinckaers does however say here that our ability to elude the attraction of the highest good (in this life) ultimately lies in a 'defect in our spiritual faculties'.[32] Not only can the intellect be deceived, but the will can weaken in the face of the effort required. Here there lies a hint that the freedom of exercise possessed in this life is a defect in freedom lost to the more perfect freedom of the next. Indeed Pinckaers has in fact already made it clear that the freedom to sin is no part of the essence of freedom.

The 'freedom to sin', then, has a place in a morality of excellence very different from the place it possesses in a morality of indifference. Pinckaers had already noted that because freedom of indifference is defined as a choice between contraries, it is implied that the choice between good and evil is a first form of choice. The power to sin is thus of the very essence of freedom conceived thus.[33] However, in terms of the

[31] *Sources*, pp. 396–7.
[32] *Sources*, p. 397.
[33] *Sources*, p. 374.

freedom for excellence, the ability to sin is a *lack* of freedom. Pinckaers mentions not only the moral life here, but also the arts, examples of which had introduced the whole notion of freedom for excellence. In those examples, the ability to make mistakes was quite distinct from the artistic freedoms that were being developed. Indeed the more the abilities to play the piano and speak a foreign language were perfected, the more the ability to make mistakes was excluded. Pinckaers says that the ability to commit faults in the moral life as well as in the arts is 'lessened if not eliminated by progress'. So the ability to sin is only 'accidental' to freedom, even though it is part of the human condition in this world.[34] He confirms from various texts that this is St Thomas's view[35] (and we might add that it was also Anselm's, as we have seen in previous chapters). In contrast then to the imperfection of the ability to sin, the greatest freedom is God's: God who is impeccable, fully creative, with no interior limitations on his powers.[36]

Here we have Pinckaers's hints at how the two freedoms might apply to eschatology. Freedom of indifference requires a lot of work to explain the difference between the moral freedom of this world (where the ability to sin is of the essence of freedom) and the freedom of the blessed and of the impeccable God. Pinckaers says that he wonders whether on this view, human beings must always renounce an essential part of their freedom (that is, freedom of indifference) on approaching God.[37] In contrast, in terms of the freedom for excellence, the nearer one approaches to God through moral progress, the more one's inclination to sin has been lessened. Pinckaers suggests that such a one has grown more in full freedom, sharing in the divine freedom itself, and I shall develop this suggestion in Chapter 8. The blessed thus lose none of their freedom, Pinckaers suggests, but rather through grace become supremely free as God is free: 'They are free as to truth and goodness and enjoy perfect knowledge and a very pure love, which they express in praise

---

[34] *Sources*, p. 376.
[35] *Sources*, pp. 338–9, citing e.g. *Summa Theologiae*, Ia., q. 62, a. 8 ad 3 (IX, pp. 240–1).
[36] *Sources*, p. 376.
[37] *Sources*, p. 374.

of the works of divine grace in the world and in humanity.'[38] And we can add that this 'freedom for excellence' will be no mere ad hoc solution produced to face the charge that impeccability seems to reduce the freedom of the blessed. 'Freedom for excellence' derives from a more radical examination of the meaning of human freedom and proves its attractiveness not only in the solution it offers for the freedom of heaven but also in what it has to offer for the moral theology of the earthly way there.

I shall have more to say of how these two freedoms relate to eschatology in the next chapter. From this chapter we can at least conclude that the freedom for excellence would seem to be more easily linked to eschatology. I say this because the moral theology based on freedom for excellence takes the moral life to be one of progress towards a goal or an end, a life which has a certain unity or continuity of its acts based on the final end of happiness to which all human beings are inclined by nature and to which their acts are directed. If God, the life of heaven, is the final goal for human beings, as Christian eschatology teaches, then the freedom for excellence would appear to be more easily related to a theology of heaven, together with an appropriate moral theology of the journey there. However, the freedom of indifference would appear not to be so easy to relate to eschatology. If it is of the essence of freedom to be able to reject happiness, one's ultimate goal, then it is by no means clear how a theology of heaven can be based on this freedom without encountering significant tensions. In the final chapter, I shall assess, in the light of Pinckaers's distinction between the two freedoms, the eschatologies of some of those theologians whose work I have mentioned in previous chapters.

[38] *Sources*, p. 376.

7

Two Freedoms, Two Eschatologies?

Pinckaers's two systems of moral theory based on two different notions of freedom have suggested that the two different notions of freedom might also be linked to two different eschatologies. Each eschatology would also be linked to the moral theory derived from the same view of freedom, whether the freedom of indifference or the freedom for excellence. Given that the freedom for excellence is closely linked to happiness and an ultimate end in morals, it may be supposed that a theology of final beatitude will cohere very easily with this notion of freedom and its system of morality. The freedom for excellence may be supposed to settle very easily into a bliss which is perpetual and without the possibility of its loss by sin. In contrast, the freedom of indifference may be expected to cohere not so easily with a theology of final beatitude, since it is of the very essence of the freedom of indifference to be able to reject such beatitude in every circumstance, defying indeed the very notion that this beatitude *must* be a final one. Presupposing such a typology of two freedoms linked to two eschatologies, I shall examine each of the theologians we have encountered in the previous chapters, and see how their theologies of freedom and heavenly impeccability may be placed with respect to this typology.

Donnelly's theology is easily placed. It seems to me that it is a perfect instantiation of an eschatology which is the logical consequence of a radical freedom of indifference. It is because he takes freedom to be such a freedom of indifference that Donnelly is led to conclude that heaven, since it involves freedom, must involve the real possibility of moral evil. So in heaven the moral struggle continues, and it is possible that heaven may be lost and then possibly regained. Where freedom of indifference is allowed its full implications, heaven loses its intrinsic finality. It is not a goal in which human beings come to their final rest, but somewhere from which they can *depart*. Where freedom of indifference is taken to its logical conclusion, eschatology is hardly of the 'last' things at all, but of a state that is in principle always temporary. Since he does not wish to be unorthodox, Donnelly is concerned to argue that his position of a heaven in principle temporary is that of orthodox Christianity, though, as we have seen, in this he fails.

There does appear then to be a tension between the full implications of the freedom of indifference and the orthodox notion of heaven as a final homeland of happiness that can never be lost. Consequently we might expect that any theology, which is both based on the freedom of indifference and moreover attempts to cling to an orthodox eschatology, will suffer internal tensions and appear unstable. Such a theology will find itself in the position of either having to abandon orthodoxy and capitulate to Donnelly's view, or if it does not wish to give up either pole in the tension, it will have to reduce the freedom of indifference in some way. William of Ockham provides a clear example of this tension. His notion of freedom is the same as Donnelly's, the freedom of indifference. However, while Donnelly strays from the orthodox view of heaven, Ockham maintains it. This means, however, that he must face the tension between the freedom of indifference and the fact that the blessed cannot sin. Ockham's radical freedom of indifference would suggest that the blessed can sin, and Ockham has to accept, on his own logic, that this is the case. So he resolves the tension by declaring that in heaven the blessed are not left to their own freedom, but that God is the total cause of their beatific act of will. In other words, the tension is overcome by suppressing the freedom that is the very cornerstone of so much of Ockham's philosophical and theological project. In view of the importance of this freedom to Ockham in general, its final suppression can hardly make Ockham's system a satisfying one.

Scotus's solution is perhaps a little more subtle, yet it still manifests the same basic tension as Ockham's. Scotus's view of freedom bears a great deal of similarity to Ockham's, though Scotus does not go so far as to say that the blessed can nill God. They can, however, not will him, though I suggested in Chapter 4 that it is difficult to make sense of this distinction in the case of the blessed: ceasing to will him in heaven would seem to amount to nilling him. But be that as it may, the importance Scotus accords to freedom in human nature means that he must maintain the freedom of the blessed not to will God. Since, however, orthodoxy maintains that the blessed are in some sense impeccable and in some sense unable to cease to will God, Scotus has to face the familiar tension between the freedom of the blessed not to will and the fact they always continue to will. Like Ockham, Scotus deals with this tension by reducing the freedom which is in fact essential to his theological enterprise. The freedom of the blessed is reduced to a mere remote power to sin. Whereas Ockham had removed the blessed's causation of the beatific act in favour of an act totally caused by God, Scotus has God determine that the blessed's act always continue. Their freedom to sin is reduced because they never have the opportunity to exercise what now remains a mere remote power to act, one that God by his extrinsic causality will always prevent them from exercising. Once again, such a view of freedom cannot be maintained in an orthodox eschatology without in fact reducing the freedom that is so valued in Scotus's thought as a whole.

Ockham and Scotus both put forward an 'extrinsic' theory of heavenly impeccability, according to Suárez. This can be seen in the fact that the blessed remain impeccable because of God's extrinsic causality, though each theologian explains the latter in different ways. The fact that neither adopts what Suárez calls an 'intrinsic' theory of impeccability may be linked to their desire to uphold human freedom. On Scotus's view there is nothing intrinsic that does away with the human power to sin: the intrinsic power remains while the external providence of God sees that it never comes into effect. On Ockham's view there is nothing intrinsic to the blessed to secure their impeccability: in terms of their own intrinsic freedom they remain able to sin, but God does not leave them to their freedom but instead totally causes their beatific acts by his extrinsic causality. Since the extrinsic theories of impeccability are linked to the desire to maintain the reality of freedom of indifference, however successfully or unsuccessfully that may be achieved, we might suppose that the intrinsic theory supported by Suárez might instead find a link with the freedom for excellence. On this view, the final and complete consummation of the freedom for excellence would of itself exclude the defect of the ability to sin. This consummation would be identified with the beatific vision, where the sight of God as the perfect good would henceforth exclude the possibility of sin. If Donnelly were to be persuaded of the orthodoxy of impeccability, it may be that such a combination of an intrinsic theory and the freedom for excellence would prove very persuasive for him, because it would maintain both orthodoxy and a notion of freedom that is arguably richer than the notion Donnelly had himself maintained. Now given that Suárez accepts an intrinsic theory of impeccability, where the blessed love God necessarily, one might then expect Suárez to claim this as a higher freedom, calling on the freedom of excellence instead of on the freedom of indifference.

However, we find no such thing. Suárez does indeed accept the orthodox notion of a perpetual heaven, as Scotus and Ockham do. And moreover, unlike Scotus and Ockham, he appears to have a more 'settled' inhabitant of heaven, given his intrinsic as opposed to extrinsic theory of both heavenly perpetuity and impeccability. On the accounts offered by Scotus and Ockham, the blessed seem slightly unstable in their place in heaven, in contrast to the intrinsic account offered by Suárez. On Ockham's account, the blessed cannot depart from heaven on account of God's extrinsic causation of the beatific acts. If they were left to themselves and their freedom, however, their place in heaven would not be so assured. On Scotus's account, the blessed again cannot depart from heaven only on account of God's extrinsic causality. If God were not to arrange things extrinsically as he does, the blessed could then exercise their continuing power to sin. So again their place in heaven would not be so assured, if it were not for the intervention of God's extrinsic causality. With Suárez, however, the position of the blessed seems so much more settled, because the perpetuity of their bliss follows from their beatific acts. Even with God 'leaving them to themselves' or however one of the two Franciscans might want to put it, the blessed still have no possibility of leaving heaven, such is the cleaving of their minds and wills to God. On Suárez's view, the blessed are more settled in their final state because, seeing God, they necessarily love him and cannot sin.

But what Suárez fails to do is to link this intrinsic causation of impeccability with the freedom for excellence. Suárez might have claimed that freedom, understood thus, easily finds its goal in this unswerving adherence of intellect and will to God, with the lesser ability to sin excluded. But, as we saw in Chapter 2, Suárez comes nearer to Scotus and Ockham in his understanding of freedom. So when Suárez comes to ask whether there is still freedom in the blessed, he raises and dismisses as equivocation the assertions of Augustine and Anselm that the blessed are *more free*. Such assertions are themselves suggestive of the freedom for excellence, but for Suárez, the proper meaning of freedom is undoubtedly the freedom of indifference, even if it is not so radical as to be able to nill God clearly seen. The fact that the beatific vision limits the freedom of indifference in this way means that freedom in heaven has to be reduced for Suárez. Suárez maintains that there is still some freedom in heaven (one can choose whether or not to perform certain good but uncommanded secondary actions) but freedom seems to be definitely lessened in heaven, just as it was significantly reduced in the eschatologies of Ockham and Scotus. It seems that wherever freedom is understood basically in terms of indifference and the orthodoxy of impeccability is also accepted, freedom will ultimately be in some way reduced in heaven, even where impeccability is understood in the more 'settled' way of an intrinsic theory. So if someone like Donnelly were to embrace the orthodoxy of impeccability and still wish not to see freedom in heaven reduced, he or she would be unlikely to find attractive any theology that still understood freedom in terms of indifference.

In Chapter 1, I not only examined Donnelly's assertion of the freedom to sin in heaven, but also mentioned how he differed in this from the more conventional position of Richard Swinburne, which the latter expressed in his *Providence and the Problem of Evil* (1998). I recorded how Swinburne allowed that human beings possessed the 'great good of free and efficacious choice', such that sin was 'virtually inevitable'. It was good to have the choice in this world of finally rejecting the good, so as also to be able to choose the heavenly world, which lacks (among some other goods of this world) the good of being able to choose to reject the good. In this last respect, Swinburne sounded similar to Ockham, Scotus and Suárez. In each case there was some kind of reduction of freedom in view of maintaining the orthodox doctrine of a perpetual heaven. Swinburne does indeed differ from the others in his emphasis on a *vast range* of possible goods that will be available for choice in heaven, but he does nevertheless exclude from it certain 'goods', including the good of being able to reject the good (and leave heaven). However, he differs even more from the others in his adoption of a further notion of freedom, more akin to the 'freedom for excellence'. Swinburne addresses the question of freedom and impeccability in heaven in more than one place, though he devotes only a few paragraphs in total to it. By examining what he has to say in these paragraphs, I shall now attempt to place his views within the typology I have been using in this chapter.

Swinburne does not hold that one can reject the good as such: he is no Ockhamist. Instead he believes that an agent will inevitably pursue the good, given both that he has knowledge of the good and that he is freed from 'bodily inclinations and other sources of temptation'.[1] In *The Existence of God* (1977), he had argued that a perfectly free agent, that is, one entirely free of non-rational influences, will always refrain from an action the agent judges to be 'over all a bad action' and will always do an action judged to be 'over all better to do than not to do' and which is therefore morally obligatory. This allows him to argue that God will inevitably do good. God, being perfectly free and

---

[1]   R. Swinburne, *Faith and Reason* (Oxford: Clarendon Press, 1981), p. 170.

omniscient, will always act aright and be perfectly good (in a moral sense).[2] For our purposes, this gives Swinburne's understanding of how God is impeccable. Given both his knowledge and his freedom, God is incapable of sin. Swinburne allows then that logic imposes some constraints on the possible range of actions open to God, but says that this will still leave open to him a 'very considerable choice among actions'.[3]

Swinburne does not, however, simply analyse God's freedom in terms of his having a range of choices available to him, a freedom of indifference, as it were: he also sees in God something more like Pinckaers's freedom for excellence. Nevertheless, he sometimes writes as though God were constrained in such a way that he sounds unfree. Further on Swinburne writes:

> Because of his perfect knowledge such a being would know which actions are right and wrong. Because of his perfect freedom nothing would inhibit him from avoiding what is wrong and doing what is right. He would not have chosen righteousness, but rather had it foisted upon him.[4]

Swinburne lets it sound as though God has been forced into impeccability, as though something external had constrained him. What Swinburne in fact wants to say is that a being who saw what was right and wrong 'with crystal clarity' *and was in no way diverted from it* could only wish to do what was right and would inevitably do it.[5] Such a being is considered free to follow what it knows to be right, because it is just free of any temptation that would divert it from the known true good to something less. This freedom it possesses is then a freedom from sin, but it is also a freedom to act well.

In this passage, Swinburne's aim is to argue that such a being would have reason to create beings capable of choosing whether or not to follow the good, that is, beings like us. He thinks that to have a choice whether or not to be morally good belongs to

[2]   R. Swinburne, *The Existence of God* (Oxford: Clarendon Press, 1977), p. 101.
[3]   *Existence of God*, p. 102.
[4]   *Existence of God*, p. 156.
[5]   *Existence of God*, p. 157.

an agent of *limited* freedom or knowledge. A being of limited knowledge but limitless freedom might behave badly, but only on account of ignorance, the defect being only in knowledge and not in freedom. For such a being, growth in knowledge would *inevitably* mean growth in moral goodness, since its only lack was in knowledge and not in freedom. To have a *choice* to be morally good, an agent must have *limited freedom*, being placed in a situation of sufficient knowledge to know what is right but also of temptation, a temptation which strongly pulls the agent to do something else. Such temptations have their source, Swinburne says, in a 'felt desire or natural inclination to act on it'.[6] Obvious examples are the sense-desires of food and drink, sex or sleep, but less obvious ones are for company or fame, and Swinburne identifies these as distinct from *sense-desires*.[7] For Swinburne, it is a *'sad* truth of logic' that one cannot choose one's destiny without being in a situation of temptation, and therefore of limited freedom. However, it is *good*, he concludes, for God to make some agents who have this power, though the situation of temptation it entails is for other reasons undesirable or *bad*.[8]

Swinburne allows then for growth in freedom. An agent can become a morally good being and through right choices grow in freedom and moral knowledge. Bad choices will make good choices harder the next time, and good choices will make bad choices harder the next time. Swinburne sees persistent good choices as resulting in such a growth that the agent's range of (good) choices becomes enormous, with bad choices no longer open to him. So the choice over one's destiny is not equated with 'free will' (the freedom to choose) as such. An agent with free will can have a different range of choices available. Through persistent good choices, an agent possessed of free will can grow in freedom by becoming freed of non-rational desires and becoming open to a greater range of good choices.[9] The comparison with Pinckaers's freedom for excellence is easy to make: the practised musician becomes less capable of mistakes

---

6 *Existence of God*, p. 157.
7 *Existence of God*, pp. 157–8.
8 *Existence of God*, pp. 158–9.
9 *Existence of God*, p. 159.

and able to perform well in more and more ways. What remains for us to see is what kind of theory of impeccability Swinburne embraces, whether it is intrinsic or extrinsic. In Suárez's intrinsic theory, the vision of God as the supreme good had been sufficient knowledge to guarantee impeccability and rightness of action in the blessed. On the extrinsic theories, the beatific acts of vision and love were not in themselves sufficient, but God's extrinsic providence had somehow to guarantee the perpetuity of blessedness and exclude sin. So the intrinsic theory had the blessed more satisfactorily 'settled' in heaven in a way that an extrinsic theory did not. Does Swinburne then have the beatific acts as sufficient or insufficient for impeccability?

In *Faith and Reason* (1981), Swinburne envisages the scenario of the admission to heaven of those who are not suited to it. Heaven he takes to be primarily a 'home for good people'.[10] The life of heaven consists in its inhabitants 'performing actions of supreme worth . . . in a situation of supreme worth; and they will know that they are doing such actions and in such a situation'.[11] According to Christian theology, Swinburne says, the principal such heavenly activity is the enjoyment of God's friendship, which is how he describes the beatific vision. Given that God is a being of 'infinite wonder', Swinburne concludes that finite beings will take an eternity to comprehend him. However, this vision yields a surer form of knowledge than is had on earth, with a more direct grasp on reality and with God as intimately present to the inhabitant of heaven as are the inhabitant's own thoughts.[12] Now on an intrinsic theory of impeccability, the performance of these beatific acts would be sufficient for the impeccability of heaven's inhabitants. Where there is the vision of God, according to Suárez, the love of God is necessarily elicited: one who sees God with clarity possesses a right will flowing from the fact of vision. Where this is not held to be the case, theologians can conceive of the real possibility of those who see God ceasing to will him (if God did not arrange it otherwise by his extrinsic power), and this is

[10]   *Faith and Reason*, p. 147.
[11]   *Faith and Reason*, p. 148.
[12]   *Faith and Reason*, pp. 131–2.

precisely what Scotus and Ockham do. And, as we shall see, this is precisely what Swinburne seems to do too.

Swinburne hints at the situation of people unsuited to heaven admitted to this 'home for good people'. He says that the actions of heaven give rise to a 'deep happiness' *so long as the inhabitants of heaven want to be there doing those things, and not elsewhere doing something else.*[13] He appears to allow for the possibility that an inhabitant of heaven might have the (bad) desire to be elsewhere doing something else, and so would fail to experience the happiness of heaven. If someone unsuitable were admitted to the beatific vision, they would not necessarily find happiness in such perfect knowledge, the reason being that they still had openness to temptation. Note that Swinburne does not consider the possibility that possessing the beatific vision itself might *entail* a right will, the very way in which Suárez explains impeccability as intrinsic. Swinburne believes that the crucial difference between earth and heaven is the removal of 'difficulties and obstacles to success, and desires for lesser goods'.[14] However, he does not consider the possibility that the beatific vision be in itself able to remove the possibility of the success of temptation. Swinburne seems to allow that an agent with such perfect knowledge as is had in the beatific vision would not thereby have perfect freedom. Perfect freedom must be guaranteed by an otherwise-effected elimination of bad desires, such that both perfect knowledge and perfect freedom can then come together to give rise to the blessed life of heaven.

Swinburne holds that in fact only those of a certain character are admitted to heaven. Here he speaks again of his theory of 'character-formation'. Actions done on earth, where one has many opportunities to do good or evil, form one's character, normally over a period of many years. By choosing the good, one finds more opportunities to pursue good ways, and choosing the good becomes natural. By choosing, one is said to 'shift the range of moral choice'. Starting with a limited range of good or evil actions that are genuinely able to be chosen, good choices bring more possibilities for greater good next time

---

[13]   *Faith and Reason*, p. 148.
[14]   *Faith and Reason*, p. 148.

and some evil choices become 'no longer a possibility'. And conversely, bad choices widen the possibilities for future evil actions and restrict the possibility of good. Those who make good choices have thus become suited by their manner of life on earth to enjoy the life of heaven. In heaven, they will live the same sort of life, but with the obstacles to it removed.[15] However, Swinburne also wants to ask about those who have followed the good, but with 'imperfect dedication'. This he does in an appendix on the 'after-life'. Swinburne considers that such people would find heaven 'tough going' before it became enjoyable, unless God were to mould their characters and suppress their desires for lesser goods.[16]

Swinburne allows the genuine possibility of what he takes to be the Protestant view, namely that God will *immediately* 'get rid of' these lesser desires at death and admit these people to heaven.[17] He also considers the Catholic notion of purgatory here, but finds it difficult on account of its irreversible nature, which would eliminate any continuing choices on the part of the agent whether to undergo the process of purging or not. His alternative 'Catholic' proposal also envisions the possibility of such agents by free choice 'backsliding' but never losing the possibility of choosing the good, even if they have to remain in this state for ever on account of always yielding to desires for lesser goods.[18] Swinburne allows that a Christian might choose between this view and the Protestant view that evil desires are all simply removed by God at death, or just remain agnostic on the matter. Swinburne himself goes on to hypothesise that a further class, namely those without fixity of dedication to the good but some good will nonetheless, might be enabled to form their characters after death either way, but ultimately counsels a 'healthy agnosticism'.[19] What is beyond question for Swinburne is the supposition that all evil desires must be first removed if someone is to enjoy heaven. This removal would be effected by God's extrinsic power, and would seem to be what

[15] *Faith and Reason*, pp. 148–9.
[16] *Faith and Reason*, p. 168.
[17] *Faith and Reason*, p. 168.
[18] *Faith and Reason*, pp. 168–9.
[19] *Faith and Reason*, p. 169.

is crucial in guaranteeing the impeccability of the blessed. It is informative to compare Swinburne here with Aquinas, who distinguishes between right will as necessary for beatitude *antecedently* and right will as necessary for beatitude *concomitantly*.[20] Rectitude of will is necessary prior to beatitude so that one is rightly ordered to the end of beatitude; this Swinburne would endorse. However, rectitude of will is also *concomitantly* necessary to beatitude, because such a will follows necessarily from the fact that God is seen as the supreme good: whatever God loves is thus loved in subordination to him. For this distinct concomitant right will Swinburne seems to have no place, and hence there is the need for an extrinsic removal of bad desires and thus an extrinsic theory of impeccability.

In the same appendix Swinburne asks whether it is 'plausible to suppose that a good God would keep permanently in Heaven those who on earth choose the good way'?[21] In other words, he directly asks the question of perpetuity, and it quickly becomes focused on impeccability. He replies initially that it is the 'traditional view' that one cannot lose one's 'good character' and so one stays for ever in heaven. So one's remaining always in heaven is said to be dependent on the permanence of good character. Swinburne then goes on to say that on the 'traditional view', good character cannot be lost because, as a result of the vision of God, the inhabitant of heaven sees so clearly what is good that he has no 'temptation' to pursue any other way. In other words, on the traditional view, the vision of God brings about such a clear vision of the good that the inhabitant of heaven has no temptation to evil, retains his good character, and so remains in heaven. Here we have the position we have just encountered in Aquinas's concomitant rectitude of will. It is the same position as was held by Suárez: the intrinsic theory of perpetuity and impeccability. The vision of God itself and not some additional extrinsic providence is responsible for the perpetuity of beatitude and the exclusion of sin. In reporting this 'traditional view', has Swinburne now adopted the intrinsic theory of impeccability?

[20] *Summa Theologiae*, 1a.2ae., q. 4, a. 4 (XVI, pp. 96–101).
[21] *Faith and Reason*, p. 170.

Swinburne in fact seems to turn from this 'traditional view' to his own distinct arguments.[22] He recalls from *The Existence of God* that one who sees what is good will do good and not evil, unless he gives in to 'bodily or mental forces which are really no part of him'.[23] Swinburne understands the development of moral character to involve the making of evil desires into forces 'extrinsic' to one's adopted character.[24] So the 'extrinsic' forces in question are linked to the 'unfavourable conditions', difficulties and obstacles, desire for lesser goods, and 'evil desires' of which we have already spoken. Swinburne says that an inhabitant of heaven, who had reached this position through his good choices in spite of such 'forces', could only choose the bad again *if* God exposed him to such forces once more. Swinburne says that the traditional answer (that an inhabitant of heaven never departs from heaven) follows from the 'claim that God does not allow an inhabitant of Heaven to be so exposed'. Swinburne thinks this claim to be not implausible, because while there is good in the fact that heaven is the object of a choice of destiny made over a considerable period of time, there is also good in good choices leading to a final removal of temptation.

I suggest that in his appeal to his own arguments, Swinburne is differing from 'the traditional view' that impeccability follows from the beatific vision as such, although he by no means makes this absolutely clear. Certainly he wishes to give the 'traditional answer' that those in heaven remain there permanently. However, in giving his own arguments for this answer, he states his own view that one 'who sees what is good will only do what is bad if he gives in to bodily or mental forces which are really no part of him'. We should notice that Swinburne allows for the possibility that one who sees what is good (including one who sees God) can nevertheless do what is bad on account of giving in to these 'forces'. On the traditional account, such forces would be eliminated by the vision of the supreme good

[22] *Faith and Reason*, pp. 170–1.
[23] *Faith and Reason*, p. 171.
[24] Cf. R. Swinburne, 'A Theodicy of Heaven and Hell', in A. J. Freddoso (ed.), *The Existence and Nature of God* (Notre Dame, IN: University of Notre Dame Press, 1983), p. 54, n. 19.

itself, but because Swinburne allows that one who sees it can nevertheless do evil by giving in to these 'forces', he seems to suppose that these 'forces' must be eliminated by some means other than the beatific vision itself. Swinburne's statement that one 'who sees what is good' and can nevertheless do evil on account of certain 'forces' seems to cover not only human knowledge of the good on earth, but also such knowledge in the beatific vision of heaven. It is thus that he allows that an inhabitant of heaven could 'choose the bad again, if God allows him to be exposed to such forces again'.

In other words, should God thus expose the blessed, they would once more have the possibility of sinning, even though they possessed the clarity of knowledge of the good afforded by the beatific vision. So those in heaven are impeccable on account of a removal of the 'forces' in question, additional to the clear knowledge of the good afforded by vision. In this way Swinburne derives the 'traditional answer' he requires, namely that heaven is a permanent state, not from the 'traditional view' of the beatific vision, but from 'the claim that God does not allow an inhabitant of Heaven to be so exposed'. In other words, God will see to it that there is no possibility of sin occurring, because he sees to it that there are no difficulties or obstacles arising for those in heaven, no evil desires, no desire for lesser goods. But this removal of such forces is something additional to the beatific vision and does not derive from the vision itself. It is this removal then that ultimately accounts for the continuing stability of moral character and so for the permanence of heaven. Indeed, in a later essay Swinburne speaks of the removal of these forces in the next life without mention of the beatific vision at all.[25]

How then might we fit Swinburne into the typology used so far in this chapter? Donnelly's rejection of the eschatological finality of heaven was shown to be the logical consequence of his adoption of the centrality of the freedom of indifference. Indifference and a rejection of final beatitude go together. Others who held to the centrality of indifference, but who wanted to maintain eschatological finality, attempted the latter by an

---

[25] Swinburne, 'A Theodicy of Heaven and Hell', p. 54, n. 19.

extrinsic theory of impeccability, in which the inhabitants of heaven would remain unsettled in their state were it not for God's extrinsic action. In Scotus's case the blessed were determined not to discontinue their beatific act of love, and in Ockham's case God became the total cause of the beatific act. Swinburne also has this same extrinsicism: the blessed are only settled in their heavenly state by the extrinsic removal of all sources of temptation. To this Donnelly would have objected that their freedom was in fact being removed, since the blessed are no longer able to sin. Swinburne has opened the possibility of making a reply in Scotist terms: the blessed retain a remote ability to sin, which is however unable to pass into act on account of God's removal of all sources of temptation. Swinburne, it seems, would however make no attempt to defend the freedom of the blessed in such terms. Swinburne's commitment is not to freedom conceived in this way but rather in terms of something like Pinckaers's freedom for excellence. The blessed are more free in that they are freer of temptation and thus also freer to pursue the good in a rational way. Swinburne thus combines freedom for excellence with an extrinsic theory of impeccability, just as Suárez had combined freedom of indifference with an intrinsic theory of impeccability. Both these combinations seem to go against what is suggested by the typology we have been using, namely, that the freedom of indifference is most easily linked with the rejection of eschatology and the freedom for excellence with a full embracing of a more 'settled' eschatology.

Now Scotus and Ockham both embraced their extrinsicisms because they wished to defend the freedom of the blessed in terms of the freedom of indifference. Swinburne, however, embraces a comparable extrinsicism not because he wishes to defend the freedom of the blessed in terms of indifference – he does not – but simply because he does not embrace the more powerful theology of the beatific vision offered by Aquinas and Suárez. As we have seen, such a theology, where the beatific vision itself gives rise to perpetuity and impeccability, is more satisfying in that it has the blessed settled in their knowledge and love of the supreme good, without the *extra* requirement of any *further* extrinsic divine activity to keep them settled. But again, as we have seen, Suárez failed to link this intrinsic theory of impeccability to the richer freedom for excellence, just as Swinburne fails to link the freedom for excellence to the more satisfactory intrinsic theory of impeccability. It is to the linking of this more satisfactory theory of impeccability with the richer freedom for excellence, a theology I propose as more attractive to those who wish to accept both the orthodoxy of impeccability and the continuing value of freedom in heaven, that I shall now turn in my final chapter.

8

There Will Be Free Will in Heaven

In its maturity in this life, freedom for excellence can be expected to be characterised by the ability to act in an excellent manner, the fact that one is master of human acts of great value in all the situations that may arise in the life of the human community. Such acts are truly performed as one's own in view of one's ultimate goal. This goal is something one has recognised and appropriated for oneself, and in view of it all one's acts form a continuous and unitary narrative of a human life focused on its ultimate fulfilment. All one's faculties, ideas, desires and emotions are together directed to this higher end, to the benefit of one's own being and all those with whom one comes into contact. Because this ultimate goal is revealed to be one that exceeds the capacities of human nature – it is a heavenly union of knowledge and love with the infinite God – this freedom is in the final analysis the fruit of God's grace, of his gift of himself and of the gifts of the Spirit, of 'theological' virtues which exceed human capacities and direct human beings to God. Arrival at this ultimate goal might then be expected to herald arrival at the perfection and consummation of this freedom. The indwelling of the Holy Spirit in grace leads to the presence of God's essence as the clearly seen object of knowledge and love. The theological virtues lead to their perfection in themselves or their perfection by the presence of something which surpasses them: charity being perfected in itself, hope being replaced by possession of what was hoped for, and faith by the sight of what was formerly believed in. It is here that growth in freedom of excellence leads, and so it is here that one might expect to

119

find the exercise of this freedom in all its fullness, in the beatific vision of God, where the ultimate end is at last attained.

Of its very nature as a freedom for excellence, this freedom also works to exclude those actions which fall short of excellence. The ability to sin is no part of the freedom for excellence, but is gradually eliminated, just as the attainment of a new musical or linguistic freedom reduces the capacity for error and mistakes. But Catholic faith does not allow for a complete sinlessness in this life, unless it be by a special grace, as is believed to be the case (though in different ways) of Jesus and Mary. The life of grace and virtue, even in those of the maturity of which we have been speaking, is not supposed by Catholics to guarantee something even approaching absolute impeccability. On the one hand, grace may be sufficient for one to avoid a sin so serious that one has thereby placed one's ultimate end in something other than God, where it truly lies. On the other, one cannot hope not to fall at some time into faults of a lesser nature that do not in fact displace God as one's final end. As long as God remains unseen, sin will remain possible even for those who accept on faith that he is their final end: until then they are in their defective freedom always able to consider him as unsuitable for them in some respect, and turn to some other good. But in heaven they will have clear knowledge that he is without any defect or unfittingness for them.

On this view, freedom and impeccability will coincide. Where freedom reaches its perfection in heaven, sin will be altogether excluded; and when sin has been completely excluded, one is perfectly free in view of one's end, the end now already attained. For the perfection of freedom for excellence, a fresh eschatological gift is required. It is one prepared for by the life of faith, and thus faith is indeed the beginning of this eternal life, grace the seed of glory. But the perfection of this life is not guaranteed without the eschatology of heaven: not the beginning of eschatology where the Christ and the Spirit inaugurate the kingdom of God in this world, but the consummation of that eschatological kingdom where God is seen as he really is. In Chapter 7, we saw that Swinburne placed this new intervention in two things additional to the perfected characters of the saved: the perfect knowledge of the beatific vision and the removal of all sources of temptation. On St Thomas's account, however, we saw that the vision itself was sufficient to establish the soul (in fact disposed in this life by an antecedent rectitude of will) in a new concomitant rectitude of will, and thus to remove the possibility of sin for ever. In this supremely 'settled' eschatology, where impeccability and perpetuity enjoy an intrinsic cause, it is the very same thing that guarantees the perfection of freedom as guarantees impeccability, namely, the beatific vision. Since the greater freedom is, the more sin is excluded, freedom at its perfection will mean complete impeccability. There ought then to be no real tension between freedom and impeccability, and it is the vision of God that establishes both.

To what extent though may the act of beatitude turn out to be not free but necessary? By this I am asking whether the blessed are *free* in their seeing God, whether they are free to turn away from him. To answer this question, first I shall look at Aquinas's question in the *Summa Theologiae* whether happiness, once had, can be lost: *utrum beatitudo habita possit amitti?*[1] St Thomas, following the convention we encountered in Chapter 1, attributes to Origen the error that one can become unhappy again after having attained to ultimate happiness. He gives two reasons why this Origenist view is erroneous. The first is that beatitude, as the perfect and sufficient good it is, must set human desire at rest and exclude every evil. Thomas sees it as part of the natural desire of human beings to want to hold on to the good that they have, and be assured of holding on to what they have. The alternative is that either they will be troubled by the fear of losing their good, or by the sorrow of the knowledge that they will lose it – in other words, they can never have perfect beatitude at all, if they continue to have such troubles. So Thomas concludes that the blessed must have assurance that they will never lose their beatitude, untroubled by the fear that they might lose it or the sorrow that they will indeed lose it. St Thomas considers the possibility that this assurance might be a false opinion: the blessed might be *falsely* assured in their opinion that they will never lose beatitude and

---

[1] *Summa Theologiae*, 1a.2ae., q. 5, a. 4 (XVI, pp. 124–9).

so be without fear and sorrow, being in fact able to lose their beatitude all along. But this St Thomas dismisses: if the blessed were in error, then they would not have been truly blessed in the first place. The false is the evil of the intellect, the good of which is the *true*. So someone with such a false opinion concerning their happiness would not be truly happy. We might add that such a one would be deserving of our pity, and it is difficult to see how someone deserving our pity could be called truly blessed. Consequently the blessed have as part of their perfect happiness the true assurance that they will never lose their happiness.

St Thomas's first argument was based on considerations of the notion of happiness in general. His second argument is based on that in which perfect beatitude specifically consists, namely, vision of the divine essence. Thomas states that it is impossible for anyone who already sees the divine essence to wish not to see it. The reason for this is that with every good that one possesses yet wishes to be without, that good must either be insufficient (with us desiring something more sufficient instead) or it must have something 'unsuitable' (*inconveniens*), some 'unfittingness' attached to it (so that it becomes wearisome for us). It is only on the basis of such things, Thomas thinks, that one would wish to be without a certain good that one already has. The vision of the divine essence, however, fills the soul with all good things, on account of the fact that it unites the soul to the source of all goodness. Moreover, there is nothing unfitting attached to the divine essence. St Thomas has already quoted from the Book of Wisdom in support of how the vision of God satisfies the soul (7:11), and now in support of his second point he cites: *her conversation has no bitterness, and her company no tediousness* (8:16). The point seems to be that the divine essence contains no lack of perfection such that it could possibly be perceived by one who sees that essence as somehow 'inconvenient' to the one who sees it. There is nothing unsuitable for one in the supreme goodness, which is clearly seen for what it is. So Thomas can conclude that one who sees God could never turn away from him.

Beatitude might also be lost, it might be supposed, not by the soul turning away from God but by God turning away from the soul. So St Thomas also asks whether beatitude could be lost by God removing it. The answer is no, on account of God's justice. The removal of a good possessed is without doubt a punishment. Because of that, God, being a just judge, will only remove it on account of some fault. But those who see God have a concomitant rectitude of will, as Thomas has already shown and we have already seen. Because they have such a will they cannot sin, and on account of that cannot be justly punished. In other words, once impeccability is established by the beatific vision, nothing can follow on account of which the justice of God could remove beatitude. Moreover, no other agent has the power to break the union that exists between the minds of the blessed and the divine essence, because these minds have been raised to God above every other being. Having excluded all these ways in which beatitude might be thought to be able to be lost, Thomas concludes that it seems 'unfitting' (*inconveniens*) that human beings should pass from being happy to wretched and vice versa: such vicissitudes of time can only be for what is subject to time and change, and the blessed are no longer so subject.

Such is St Thomas's case for the happiness of the blessed never being able to be lost. In Chapters 4 and 5, we saw a different point of view put by Scotus and Ockham. Both of course agreed that beatitude would *in fact* never be lost, Ockham by the final suspension of that radical indifference he attributed to human freedom, and Scotus in such a way that he tried to maintain a continuity of the free nature of human beings between this life and the next, a freedom retained though never exercised. Their objections to the kind of view propounded by Thomas thus proceed, at least in part, from their view of human freedom as fundamentally involving choice, involving on Ockham's part the freedom to nill God (a freedom in fact suppressed in heaven), but on Scotus's part the freedom to cease to will him (a retained freedom God prevents from being exercised).

However, Scotus also has concerns about maintaining divine freedom: it is always *God* who freely wills to hold human beatitude in existence, and St Thomas would of course never deny that God was the ultimate cause of human beatitude, along with all else that is good in creation. But, following St Thomas's argument, to be truly happy the blessed must necessarily be granted assurance that their beatitude is perpetual, and it does not seem to derogate from the freedom of God that he freely grant such security to the blessed. There seems to be no reason to think that God's free granting of such a gift must put the created gift in some competition with him as the cause of perpetuity, such that the fact of his own freedom in granting it is excluded. The blessed know it as part of their beatitude that God will always preserve their beatitude, otherwise they could not be said to be truly blessed at all, being in fear, sorrow or ignorance. So one can argue with St Thomas from the fact that the blessed are truly blessed to the fact that their blessedness cannot be lost, while agreeing that the ultimate cause of the fact that it cannot be lost is of course the same God who causes them to be blessed at all. If, though, we were to imagine a scenario in which it were part of God's freedom to *remove* blessedness once given, as Scotus does, we must surely conclude that what was in fact once given can hardly have been true beatitude, since the supposedly blessed would have been falsely assured of perpetuity at the very least. The suggestion that God thus cannot give beatitude and then remove it should not, however, be characterised as a limitation on God's freedom. The limitation lies not in God but in the very nature of perfect beatitude: if it is not somehow of assured perpetuity, it is simply not *perfect* beatitude. But God from his own freedom freely imparts (perpetual) beatitude to those whom he graciously renders worthy of it.

We return then to the objection that wants to maintain the reality of finite human freedom as necessarily involving the power not to will God (and so sin). This freedom not to will God, having once willed him beatifically, is seen by Scotus as the *continuity* of the nature of the blessed with their nature before they received blessedness. Scotus rejects any view that renders the blessed unfree not to will God, partly on account of the fact that that would allegedly undermine the continuity of (free) nature. This charge can be brought against Aquinas's arguments that the blessed cannot choose to depart from the vision of God because there is nothing greater for them to will than that which contains all goodness and excludes all evil. For Scotus, the finite freedom of the blessed must triumph over all apparent limitations on their freedom, precisely because the nature of the blessed must remain the same (and I have suggested that, for Scotus, if it does not, the blessed would have departed from their own natural finitude and trespassed on the infinite freedom which can belong only to the divine nature and not to finite human nature). This is a continuity of human nature understood in terms of the freedom to choose to will or not to will.

However, if we want to look at matters from the perspective of the freedom for excellence, we might perhaps see that Aquinas's view that blessedness can never be lost in fact bears witness to a more profound view of the continuity of human nature, joined to a more profoundly 'settled' eschatology. In Chapter 6, we saw how, while the freedom of indifference was something simply given and static, the freedom for excellence was of its very nature dynamic and made for growth. Hence the continuity properly affirmed of the freedom of indifference will be a static one, while the continuity properly affirmed of the freedom for excellence will be a dynamic one, a continuity-in-growth. For one who champions the freedom of indifference, freedom in heaven must be exactly the same as that on earth, the freedom to turn away from God. For one who accepts the freedom for excellence, it matures in such a way that it becomes more open to act well in more and more ways, at the same time excluding more and more the defect of being able to commit faults. So in heaven we have the consummation of the freedom for excellence: one knows the good in such a way that one cannot will to lose it and hence one can no longer turn from God and sin. There may be discontinuity here – in heaven one cannot sin whereas on earth one still could – but this discontinuity is perfection of a growth in freedom of excellence, and hence is the consummation of a dynamic continuity where one remains permanently settled in the security of heaven.

This continuity of dynamic growth in freedom may be better grasped when we recall how Pinckaers described the freedom for excellence as rooted in the natural inclinations of human nature. Freedom was not fundamentally opposed to nature, but virtue and so on were proper developments of the natural inclinations of human beings. At root, St Thomas sees human nature, like all natures, as of itself inclined to its own flourishing and fulfilment, to its good. All human beings by nature want to be happy, and it is this that lies at the root of all their actions and of their growth in freedom. So in the consummation of this growth that we find in heaven, we see the fulfilment of this natural desire by the gift of God himself in the beatific vision. The soul, now clearly beholding the supreme good, can only refuse to delight in it by contradicting what is so fundamental to its nature, its natural inclination to the good and happiness. The blessed can only turn away from God by going against what is in fact so natural to them that it cannot be negated: this very desire for the good and happiness. From this perspective, it is those who would assert that we could nill or not will God clearly seen who would be in the business of seeing our nature destroyed. Ockham sees it as in fact fundamental to our nature that we have the freedom of indifference to nill the good, and Scotus sees it as fundamental that we can choose not to will our beatitude. But on the kind of account of nature held by Aquinas, such views are fundamental denials of our nature, and once our nature is properly understood, its heavenly impeccability can be clearly seen as the true fulfilment of a dynamic growth in freedom that preserves our nature just as it fulfils it: grace does not destroy nature but perfects it.

This discussion has brought us to St Thomas's teaching that we necessarily will our beatitude. In Chapter 3, I compared Scotus and Aquinas on this issue, and I concluded there that both agree we necessarily will our happiness in terms of specification. In other words we cannot nill our happiness. Again I concluded that both agree we are nevertheless free here in terms of the exercise of the act: although we cannot nill our happiness, we need not always be making the act of willing it. We have also seen how Suárez and other commentators on Aquinas had a difference of opinion here on how to interpret him. Did this freedom of exercise apply to the beatific vision or not? Suárez thought that it did, so that Aquinas proffered a teaching Suárez thought mistaken: in heaven we are free to cease exercising the act of beholding God. Other commentators, however, thought that Aquinas's teaching on freedom of exercise applied only to this life. The fact that Aquinas also states that we cannot turn from God clearly seen to some supposedly more sufficient good surely implies that in heaven we are just not free to cease to behold God in the way that we are free on earth to stop thinking about him or our happiness. The ability to turn away from God is excluded by the freedom for excellence that comes with the beatific vision. So we have to conclude against Suárez that Aquinas did not think one could cease to look on God, once he was already clearly seen. The text in question applies then only to the present life.[2]

A further question, however, is whether it is freely rather than necessarily that the blessed look on God in the first place. Does the fact that the blessed are not free to look away from him imply that it is unfreely that they first beheld him? Or is it possible that the blessed look freely, and once having looked are no longer free to look away? The question is relevant because the fact that one is not free to look away from God, once he is seen, might be taken to imply that God somehow forces himself on the soul: if one cannot turn away, perhaps one *had* to turn towards. It might be supposed that God puts himself in the line of vision, unlooked for, and the soul, mesmerised by what is forced on its sight, is compelled into the vision of God and unable to turn its sight elsewhere. In fact, it is the whole point of placing human beings in a state of imperfect knowledge and freedom – where they are able to sin and able not to sin – that they there have the choice of the perfect freedom of not being able to sin. Those who are admitted to the beatific vision are precisely those who have their sight trained on looking out for God. It is those who die in a state of grace (those who are properly disposed to God as their final end, rather than to something less) who are the ones admitted to heaven. So those in whose line of sight God places himself are precisely those who are properly disposed to be looking out for him, those who have themselves freely chosen (or in the case of infants, those who had the choice made for them) to be trained

---

[2]   *Summa Theologiae*, 1a.1ae., q. 10, a. 2 (XVII, pp. 86–91). Cf. *De Malo*, q. 6, a. un. (XXIII, pp. 145–53; ET: pp. 551–64).

on looking out for him. So it is not that anyone is compelled to look on God against his or her will: it is only those who are willing who are shown him. But once they have looked, they can no longer look away.

It is now time to ask what role might remain for free will in heaven, given that we have adopted an account of freedom as freedom for excellence rather than as freedom of indifference. If we have rejected a supremely radical freedom of indifference, to see God as he really is can no longer fall under free choice. But what then *can* fall under freedom of choice, once we adopt freedom for excellence instead? As we saw in Chapter 6, the adoption of freedom for excellence by no means implied no role for free choice, but simply meant that choice was not the radical reality someone like William of Ockham supposed it to be. In Pinckaers's examples of a musical freedom and a linguistic freedom, even as the ability to make mistakes is excluded by growth in these freedoms, so one is enabled more and more to choose different pieces to perform with ease and form more and more sentences at choice within the constraints of the rules of grammar. So this suggests a continuing role for free choice, but not one so radical that the will can choose to nill the ultimate good. But with freedom of choice contextualised within the more basic inclination of human nature to its happiness, and that same inclination now fulfilled in heaven, what in fact is left open for free willing? If the sight of the perfect good cannot be brought to an end, the will has always been able to turn away from a particular good, because as particular it could be perceived as lacking good in some respect. But why should the blessed, who see the perfect good, will one that is imperfect? Moreover, St Thomas also associates 'choice' (*electio*) with ways or means to an end: one can make a free choice of means in order to attain one's end.[3] But when the ultimate end is already attained, what need can there be for a free choice of ways to an end?

The fact of a continuing free will in the blessed, and moreover a more powerful one, is affirmed by St Thomas when he asks in

---

[3]   *Summa Theologiae*, 1a.2ae., q. 13, a. 3 (XVII, pp. 128–31). See also 1a., q. 83, a. 4 (XI, pp. 246–9).

the *Summa Theologiae* whether a beatified angel can sin.[4] As intellectual creatures their supernatural beatitude consists in the same operation as that of human beings: the vision of God. Given that God's essence is the very essence of goodness, Thomas can conclude that the angel who sees God is ordered to him just as those who do not see God are ordered to the general form of goodness. Just as the good as such is the object of the will – no one can will without aiming at something good in some respect, even if it is illusory – so the blessed angel cannot will or act without aiming at God: *angelus igitur beatus non potest velle vel agere, nisi attendens ad Deum*. The argument concludes that, given that the angel cannot will or act *except in this manner*, it cannot sin. If all its willing and actions are aimed at God clearly seen, it cannot sin. Two of the objections Thomas puts to this conclusion, however, are concerned with opposing the impeccability of blessed angels on the ground of their freedom.

The first of these two objections[5] is based on the angel's rational freedom for opposites, which might be expected to be present in the beatific vision as it was beforehand. Given that the will is a rational power, and a rational power is referred to opposites, the rational will of the beatified angel must be able to be referred to both good *and* evil. Thomas replies that the rational powers are only referred to opposites in those things to which they are not naturally inclined. Those things to which they are naturally inclined are certain naturally known principles in the case of the intellect, and the good as such in the case of the will. So the beatified angels have no tendency to opposites in regard to God himself, given that in the beatific vision they see him to be the very essence of goodness. Nevertheless, in other things they are referred to opposites: there are many things that they can choose to do or not do, although these can never be sinful, because the choices in question are always properly ordered to God.

The second of the objections[6] sees freedom as *diminished* by impeccability. It belongs to human 'free will' (*liberum arbitrium*)

4   *Summa Theologiae*, 1a., q. 62, a. 8 (IX, pp. 238–41).
5   *Summa Theologiae*, 1a., q. 62, a. 8, ad 2 (IX, pp. 240–1).
6   *Summa Theologiae*, 1a., q. 62, a. 8, ad 3 (IX, pp. 240–1).

to be able to choose good and evil, and so if angels are not to have their freedom lessened by beatitude, they too must be able to make this choice. In his reply, St Thomas again draws his accustomed parallel between intellect and will. In its choice of means to an end, the free will is disposed just as the intellect is disposed to conclusions drawn from principles. The end corresponds to principles, and the means to conclusions. Now, while the intellect can proceed to different conclusions according to given principles, when it proceeds to some conclusion *by passing out of the order of the principles*, that comes of its own defect. So the intellect's reasoning is *defective* when it comes to conclusions by passing out of the order of its principles. Hence, when Thomas then moves on to the case of the free will, it becomes immediately apparent that it is a *defect in freedom* for the will to be able to choose something *by turning away from the order of the end*; and such defective choice is sin. So where this defectiveness is removed from choice, the will can still choose among opposites *but with the order of the end kept in view*. This is said to be *liberum arbitrium*'s perfect freedom. So, in contrast to the objection, which would see impeccability as diminishing freedom and rendering it defective, Thomas sees peccability instead as defective freedom and impeccability as the very perfection of free will. The reason for this is that, when God is clearly seen as one's ultimate end, action cannot pass out of its order to that end. And so, Thomas says, the blessed and impeccable angels have a 'greater freedom of will' (*maior libertas arbitrii*) than do human beings in this life who can both sin and not sin.

So Thomas says more than that free choices remain in heaven. While Suárez, endorsing the static freedom of indifference, was simply to maintain that free will remains in heaven (with sin excluded from its range of choice), Thomas, endorsing the freedom for excellence, can say that the beatified have a *greater* freedom in their choosing. My question still remains, however, as to the role of this free will. It may no longer be defective and may have come to a powerful maturity, but what is the point of choosing when one has already attained one's end, that is, the perfect good, and so is presumably without desire for further ends and goods and further ways and means?

In the case of the blessed angels, one can immediately reply that by divine will they have a role in divine providence, and help guide human beings to their own share in the same blessedness. Moreover, the same can be said for beatified human souls. When St Thomas comes to consider the gift of counsel – one of the gifts of the Spirit by which he moves rational beings to act in a supernatural manner and yet freely in accordance with their nature – he asks whether this gift remains in heaven.[7] In heaven, Thomas says, God will continue to preserve in existence the knowledge he has caused in the blessed of what is to be done. Nevertheless there are also things that beatified creatures do not know, things not essential to beatitude but which concern God's providential government or guidance of the universe. These things they did not know previously but are not said to have been 'ignorant' of them in the sense that they *ought* to have known them already. So the gift of counsel is said to be in the blessed insofar as God preserves knowledge in them and further enlightens them concerning what is to be done. The blessed angels are also said to take counsel of God because they turn to him for instruction in what they must do.

It is the first objection that expresses the question I have raised about the point in the blessed choosing to act. Given that counsel is about what must be done for the sake of an end, it would seem that the gift of counsel will not remain in heaven, because there will be no end in view of which one can act, since the final end is already possessed. Not only does this objection conclude that there is no counsel in heaven, but it also implies that there is no need for free will, if acts freely willed are only done in view of attaining an end. Thomas replies that there are in fact, even in the blessed, acts that are directed to an end. More precisely these are acts that *proceed from the attainment of the end*. Thomas gives two examples, one concerning God and the other neighbour. The praise of God is one act which proceeds from attainment of the ultimate end, that is, vision of him, and another is helping others to the end attained, as in the ministrations of the angels and the prayers of the saints. It is here that Thomas locates the continuing

⁷   *Summa Theologiae*, 2a.2ae., q. 52, a. 3 (XXXVI, pp. 114–17).

contribution of counsel. In doing so, he has also suggested a way of making sense of the continuing role of free will in the blessed.

So Thomas does not hold that creatures only act so as to *obtain* an end. He holds that they always act in view of an end, but either to obtain it or, having possessed it in some measure, to *share* it with others. He makes this observation when he enquires into God's willing things apart from himself (whom he wills necessarily as the supreme good).[8] There is a puzzle over how an agent totally fulfilled by an end attained would seek anything further. This difficulty informs the third objection to God willing things apart from himself. If God's own goodness suffices for him and completely satisfies his will, he would surely seek nothing further and so would will nothing apart from himself. The starting-point of Aquinas's own reply to the question is his observation about creatures: not only do they pursue an end, but when they attain it they rest in it and spread it out among others as far as is possible. Hence, he says, we see agents, insofar as they are perfect, producing their like. The will is responsible for communicating goodness to others as far as is possible, and this pertains especially to the divine will from which all perfection is derived in some kind of likeness. So it pertains to the divine will, which never has need to pursue any unattained good, to share its always possessed supreme goodness by communicating created likenesses of it.

So God's willing of things other than himself is a willing of ways to an end. It is not however the willing of ways to *attain* an end, but the willing of ways to *share* that end. And these ways are not necessary, but contingent: God necessarily wills himself as the highest goodness and so is necessarily blessed; but none of those ways in which God communicates his goodness have to exist. They may be *said* to be necessarily willed, but only *conditionally*, that is, given the fact that they are willed; but absolutely speaking, they are not necessarily but freely willed by God.[9] Aquinas agrees that sometimes there might in some cases be means that are necessarily willed, given that the

---

[8]   *Summa Theologiae*, 1a., q. 19, a. 2 (V, pp. 6–11).
[9]   *Summa Theologiae*, 1a., q. 19, a. 3 (V, pp. 10–17).

end cannot be attained without them, such as human beings eating in order to be healthy. Given God's perfection, however, there are no means that must necessarily be willed by him: such means could only be necessary if they imparted to him his perfection. Since they do not, they are not willed necessarily, but freely. So when Aquinas comes to ask whether God has free will, he answers in the affirmative.[10]

One objection to God having free will is that God does not will evil (Aquinas has already shown that he does not do so, on account of his perfection, or at least that he does not will evils per se), and since free will is said to be that faculty by which good and evil are chosen, God cannot have it.[11] The first objection, however, is the authority of Jerome, which is quoted to the effect that while God is not liable to sin, all others, having free will, can be inclined either way (to sin or not to sin). Peter Lombard had already reconciled Jerome with Augustine's teaching that there was *liberum arbitrium* in God, by saying that Jerome was excluding from God free will as it exists in creatures and not as it exists in God, free will existing in God and in creatures in different ways.[12] Aquinas is a little more specific in his rebuttal of the objection: free will is denied of God not simply, but only in regard to the inclination to sin. The inclination to sin is of course, for Aquinas, a defect in free will and not part of free will as such.

The positive argument presented for the presence of free will in God is that while God wills his own goodness necessarily, other things (that is, creatures, who participate in his goodness) are not willed by him in the same necessary fashion. God is said to have free will with respect to what he wills other than necessarily. In the case of human beings, Aquinas takes it to be the case that with respect to what we will neither by necessity nor by natural instinct, we have free will. The will to be happy is referred to natural instinct and not to freedom. In the case of other animals, they are moved to act by natural instinct and never by free will: free will pertains to human animals (and

---

10 *Summa Theologiae*, 1a., q. 19, a. 10 (V, pp. 44–7).
11 *Summa Theologiae*, 1a., q. 19, a. 10, obj. 2 (V, pp. 44–7).
12 *Sentences*, bk 2, dist. 25, c. 2 (I, p. 462).

angels), but also to God. God wills himself necessarily and all else by free will. Being in perfect possession of his end, God wills to communicate that goodness by the free creation of creatures. He never acts by free will to *attain* an end, but only to *share* his perfect goodness. So when the blessed come to share in God's own beatitude, God's own knowledge and love of himself in the beatific vision, they no longer act to attain an end but now act *like God* to share the perfection attained. They do this in their worship of him and in helping others to come to the same sharing in the knowledge and love of God. So I suggest that in the beatific vision, the more powerful exercise of free will in accordance with the ultimate end attained means that the blessed imitate the freedom of God to a greater degree than they did while the end was still to be attained. Both they and God only ever act freely to communicate an end already attained.

So when God shares his own beatitude with the blessed by sharing with them his knowledge and love of himself, he gives them some share in his own freedom. They, like him, can exercise free choice without departing from the order of the ultimate end to which all their actions are referred (that is, God clearly seen). It was a defect in their freedom that, while on earth, they could depart from this order and sin, where neither by nature nor by faith could they see God. Their freedom is now more powerful in that, as it can no longer involve this departure, it can no longer give rise to sin. So God's sharing his freedom in this way is also the sharing of his own impeccability, since it is the perfection pertaining to his own freedom which he is sharing. St Thomas holds that rational creatures are able to be defective by falling away from the rectitude they ought to have.[13] It is only God who is by nature impeccable, because only God is *by nature* united to the supreme goodness as his final end, God being absolutely identical with his own goodness, his own knowledge, his own beatitude, and so on, in his absolute simplicity. The divine will is the only rule of God's act, and his act is not referred to any higher end. Rational creatures, by nature, have their wills directed to the good in general, but are

---

[13] Cf. *Summa Theologiae*, 1a., q. 63, a. 1 (IX, pp. 246–51).

not by nature united to God. They are thus capable of falling short of good action, unless they share in God's own freedom and impeccability by a gift of his grace. By human nature, human beings possess a freedom proportioned to their rational creaturehood, which allows for the ability to sin. Sharing however by grace in the divine nature, they are able to share the freedom that pertains to God, by which he and now they are unable to sin. They do this not by a knowledge of God appropriate to their own nature, but by sharing in the happiness and knowledge of God that is appropriate to *him*: this sharing is the beatific vision.

God then is impeccable by nature, but human beings (and angels) by grace, that is, by being given a share in God's nature: such is the generosity of divine grace from the perspective of St Thomas. I suggest that other views of divine grace which do not allow this same deep sharing in the divine nature do not capture the divine generosity to the same degree. We have seen that Scotus felt unwilling for impeccability to have a supernatural cause intrinsic to the human soul. Scotus wished to preserve the divine freedom as the cause of beatitude's perpetuity and impeccability, in contrast to the pretensions of any finite cause. Infinite divine freedom is consonant with God's necessary act of willing himself, but finite freedom must always involve the possibility of not willing one's ultimate end. For Scotus, finite freedom can never move beyond this possibility into what is reserved to the realm of infinite freedom, impeccability as intrinsic to the agent. If this were on the contrary allowed, there would be a confusion of God and the creature, of infinite and finite being. St Thomas, however, allows such an intrinsic impeccability by grace, where impeccability is rooted in the beatific acts of the souls (which are gifts of grace) rather than just in an extrinsic divine providence. Thomas does this by allowing a more generous share in the divine beatitude than Scotus's view of infinite and finite freedom can allow. I suggest that he is able to do this, because his distinction between creatures and the Creator is more profound than Scotus's, rooted as it is not in infinite and finite being but in a more thoroughgoing notion of divine simplicity and reinforced by the irreducibly analogical character of theological language. I have no time to defend this suggestion here, but it is not an unfamiliar one.

In conclusion, I say that there is free will in heaven. It is a more powerful freedom than freedom had on earth, because it is a more profound sharing in the divine freedom. The divine freedom is itself impeccable, because it can never depart from the ultimate end, the supreme good, as already attained, since God is in his simplicity absolutely identical with his knowing, loving and happiness. The freedom of the blessed in heaven is a sharing in this very freedom, where they by grace now exercise their freedom only within their ordering to their ultimate end, God now clearly seen through a sharing in God's own knowledge of himself. This is not, however, a sharing in God's freedom that somehow destroys their own human nature. One might suppose that, since human beings as mutable creatures are able to be defective, something natural to them is being destroyed rather than perfected by grace. However, if one looks deeper into human nature, to the natural human desire for the good and happiness, one can see that human beings can never nill or will against their happiness. So once they have become united in knowledge and love to the supreme good and are perfectly happy, they can never will against God who is now clearly seen to be the supreme good. So there is continuity in nature from earth to heaven: nature perfected and not destroyed. It is in the perfection of the natural human desire by the gift of the vision of God, that human peccability passes into graced impeccability, the defective freedom of earth into the gift of the perfect freedom of heaven. Nature would in fact be destroyed if the blessed could will against God, because they would be rejecting what they saw to be their own true happiness and so rejecting the deepest desires of their very nature.

So the blessed in heaven can no longer sin: their freedom is too perfect for that. It is perfect because they are for ever united to their ultimate end, and so their free choices will for ever be the more powerful, because, like God's, their free acts will flow from the ultimate end now possessed and from the order of which they never depart, to spread abroad the goodness and glory of God for all eternity.

Bibliography

ADAMS, M. M. 'Ockham on Will, Nature, and Morality', in P. V. Spade (ed.), *The Cambridge Guide to Ockham* (Cambridge: Cambridge University Press, 1999), pp. 245–72.

—— *William Ockham*, 2 vols (Notre Dame, IN: University of Notre Dame Press, 1987).

ANSELM, *Opera Omnia*, 6 vols (ed. F. S. Schmitt OSB, Edinburgh: Nelson, 1946–61).

—— *The Major Works* (ET: B. Davies OP and G. R. Evans, Oxford: Oxford University Press, 1998).

ARISTOTLE, *Nicomachean Ethics* (H. Rackman, Loeb Classical Library, rev. edn, vol. 19; Cambridge, MA: Harvard University Press/London: Heinemann, 1934.

AUGUSTINE OF HIPPO, *De Civitate Dei* (Corpus Christianorum, Series Latina, Turnhout, vols 47–48; ET: J. O'Meara, *Concerning the City of God Against the Pagans*; London: Penguin, 1967).

—— *Enchiridion* (CCSL, vol. XLVI; ET: B. M. Peebles in vol. 4 of *Writings of Saint Augustine* in *The Fathers of the Church: A New Translation*; New York: Cima, 1947).

—— *Contra Maximinum* (*Patrologia Latina* XLII, cols 743–814).

—— *De Trinitate* (CCSL, vol. L; ET: E. Hill OP, *The Trinity*, Brooklyn, NY: New City Press, 1991).

CROSS, R. *Duns Scotus* (New York: Oxford University Press, 1999).

DALEY SJ, B. E. *The Hope of the Early Church: A Handbook of Patristic Eschatology* (Cambridge: Cambridge University Press, 1991).

DONNELLY, J. 'Eschatological Enquiry', *Sophia* 24 (1985), pp. 16–31.

DUNS SCOTUS, JOHN. *God and Creatures. The Quodlibetal Questions* (ET: F. Alluntis OFM and A. B. Wolter OFM; Princeton and London: Princeton University Press, 1975).

—— *Opera Omnia*, 12 vols (ed. by L. Wadding OFM et al.; Lyons: Durand, 1639).

—— *Opera Omnia* (ed. by C. Balić et al.; Vatican City: Vatican, 1950–).

FLEW, A. 'Divine Omnipotence and Human Freedom', in A. Flew and A. Macintyre, *New Essays in Philosophical Theology* (London: SCM Press, 1955), pp. 144–69.

FRANK, W. A. 'Duns Scotus' Concept of Willing Freely: What Divine Freedom Beyond Choice Teaches Us', *Franciscan Studies* 42 (1982), pp. 68–89.

HICK, J. *Death and Eternal Life* (London: Macmillan, 1976).

INCANDELA, J. M. 'Duns Scotus and the Experience of Human Freedom', *The Thomist* 56 (1992), pp. 229–56.

KVANVIG, J. L. 'Heaven and Hell', in *A Companion to Philosophy of Religion*, ed. by P. L. Quinn and C. Taliaferro (Cambridge, MA: Blackwell, 1997).

LANGSTON, D. 'Did Scotus Embrace Anselm's Notion of Freedom?', *Medieval Philosophy and Theology* 5 (1996), pp. 145–59.

—— *God's Willing Knowledge: The Influence of Scotus' Analysis of Omniscience* (University Park and London: Pennsylvania State University Press, 1986).

MACKIE, J. L. 'Evil and Omnipotence', *Mind* 64 (1955), pp. 200–12.

MAHONEY SJ, J. *The Making of Moral Theology: A Study of the Roman Catholic Tradition* (Oxford: Clarendon Press, 1987).

MOONAN, L. 'Theodicy and Blissful Freedom', *New Blackfriars* 80 (1999), pp. 502–11.

ORIGEN, *De Principiis* (Die griechischen christlichen Schriftsteller, Leipzig: J. C. Hinrichs, vol. 22; ET: G. Butterworth, *On First Principles*; Gloucester, MA: Peter Smith, 1973).

LOMBARD, PETER *Sententiae in IV Libris Distinctae* (Spicilegium Bonaventurianum, 4–5; Grottaferrata: Ad Claras Aquas, 1971–81).

PINCKAERS OP, S. *The Sources of Christian Ethics* (Edinburgh: T&T Clark, 1995). *Sources* is a translation by Sr Mary Thomas Noble OP of the third edition of *Les sources de la morale chrétienne* (Fribourg: University Press, 1993).

PRENTICE, R. P. 'The Degree and Mode of Liberty in the Beatitude of the Blessed', in *Deus et Homo ad mentem I. Duns Scoti* (Rome: Societas Internationalis Scotistica, 1972), pp. 327–42.

ROGERS, K. A. *The Anselmian Approach to God and Creation* (Lampeter: Edward Mellen Press, 1997).

—— *The Neoplatonic Metaphysics and Epistemology of Anselm of Canterbury* (Lampeter: Edward Mellen Press, 1997).

SUÁREZ SJ, F. *Opera Omnia*, 28 vols (Paris: Vivès, 1856–78).

SWINBURNE, R. *Faith and Reason* (Oxford: Clarendon Press, 1981).

—— *Providence and the Problem of Evil* (Oxford: Clarendon Press, 1998).

—— *Responsibility and Atonement* (Oxford: Clarendon Press, 1989).

—— 'A Theodicy of Heaven and Hell', in A. J. Freddoso (ed.), *The Existence and Nature of God* (Notre Dame: University of Notre Dame Press, 1983), pp. 37–54.

THOMAS AQUINAS, *On the Truth of the Catholic Faith. Summa Contra Gentiles*, 5 vols (ET: C. J. O'Neil; Garden City, NY: Hanover House, 1955–7).

—— *Opera Omnia* (Rome: Leonine, 1882–).

—— *Selected Writings* (ET: R. McInerny; London: Penguin, 1998).

—— *Summa Theologiae*, 60 vols (ed. by T. Gilby OP; London: Blackfriars with Eyre and Spottiswoode, 1964–81).

WALL, G. B. 'Heaven and a Wholly Good God', *Personalist* 58 (1977), pp. 352–7.

WOLTER OFM, A. B. *Duns Scotus on the Will and Morality* (Washington, DC: Catholic University of America Press, 1986).

Index of Names